# Pages of Time

**also by Bernard Howlett**

Poetry
Seasons ISBN 978-0-9559311-0-9

Factual
The Blackbird Man ISBN 978-0-9559311-1-6

For Small Children
Grandad and the Wigglies  ISBN 978-0-9559311-2-3

# PAGES OF TIME    Bernard Howlett

**BHB**
*Bernard Howlett Books*

First published 2016
by Bernard Howlett
Beckett End, Beck Street
Hepworth, Diss
Norfolk.

Compiled & produced by SPC Printers Ltd,
Thetford, Norfolk England

# to the four winds

# Contents

**CONFLICT** **171**

# PAGES OF TIME
## in three parts

# HUMAN
# RELATIONS

# DANCING UPHILL

The first real snows of winter,
And you edge me on to make the best
Of a romp. Cloudy overhead, the
Lanes and fields beyond, impaled in
A white wilderness. Wild geese echo
The flight of the snow, echo the
Innermost pulses of nature.

Threadbare woods, each tree clad as of
Right, on just one side, as if by prior
Agreement with a mystic god, each twig,
Each branch, each trunk gilded as if
By goblins, with an inert smattering
Of flakes, on just one side,
Kissing the sleeping limbs.
An owl on guard
You say "Look here". You tweak a
Twig and a rush of snow covers me.
Cocoon like, wet, cold and wet.
You laugh.

We break along the driven track in
Conversation; or at least I try, but you
Are no longer there, no longer at my side.
I am alone in the nose chilling air.
Just a muffled snip of a snatch of a squeak
Is all the night air offers. You down a
Slippery black hole in the white night.
Up again soon.

Tracks, our tracks, their tracks, alien
Tracks sprawled across the bleak and
Wondrous universe, among the stars.
Moorhen tracks, spidery, like goblins
Fingers stroked by a delicate brush against
The snow, in a rhythmic pattern. The tracks
Of a canine. Surely not a fox. A domestic
Dog, far away from its winter clad, mountain
Orientated kin, loose on the covered plow.
Dragging its lead without permission, large,
Welded footprints follow.

The sky is black as thunder to the west,
Polluted like a kitchen to the east. City
Illuminations pollute the sky. Man wrecks
Everything. A plane drones, passengers sit
In their tin seats, in their tin can, breathing
Their tinned air.

You threaten to roll me over in the shadowy
Meadow. We dance uphill. Dancing uphill,
Like snowflakes floating uphill. You seemed
Content with dancing uphill, in the snow
Covered, unconcerned, leafless lane, where we
Left the wild, bare winter behind, to its
Chores of dragging itself back to boring
Normality.

# THESE YEARS

These years I've held you in my arms,
These years of bliss and woe;
And I will love you all my life
And never let you go.

I'll treasure all our golden days
And ev'rything we do;
And be here for you come what may
And never let you go.

Our special love is young at heart,
We know that this is so,
Whatever may the future hold
I'll go on loving you.

Old age is bound to make its mark,
The going will get slow,
But I will go on loving you
And never let you go.

Some day we'll chance the final dance
Of this we surely know,
And when we kiss our farewell kiss
I must, then, let you go.

## KNETTISHALL
## (written at the height of the cold war)


We park the car with all the rest
And take to worn and winding tracks
Across a winter wilderness,
The cold wind biting at our backs;
And up above the clouds fly high
And fieldfare chatter in the sky.

Then on a bend before our eyes,
Three local men with pointer dogs,
Are followed by two laughing boys;
They dash about and jump birch logs:
And somewhere in the silver trees
A robin seems to sing with ease.

The grasses white, sway in the gale,
The forest roars as roars the sea.
Scots pines dressed up in winter mail,
Stand dark and full of majesty;
And somewhere as we walk along,
The wind sings out its mournful song.

More people now come into view,
Chat like the fieldfares, chat with glee:
In blues and reds walk past into
A wild and windy symphony
Goldcrest voices, like tiny bells,
Ring out about the heathered dells.

The smell of pine and turpentine,
The calls of jays yet none are seen;
We pass the spot where last springtime
A dragonfly of blue and green,
Danced a jig on quivering wing,
And wished away its flush of spring.

How many lovers have there been,
Along this way, before our time?
How many foxes have been seen
Amid the heather and the pine?
The wind throws up a few rain drops,
And shakes the lofty larch-tree tops.

Wood-pigeons battle through the air,
From Norfolk and the river Thet:
They seek and search for winter fare,
They dive like smoke and pirouette
Into a dark awaiting grove,
Where ivy berries cling and move.

We pause before the forest roar,
And look up to those scattered skies,
We think, what has the world in store;
What of the earth, what of its cries
And of its creatures, great and small,
Will they, we wonder, see the fall?

Will they and we be ever lost
In mankind's ghastly holocaust
When earth may tremble like the sea;
Be robbed of all her majesty,
And there above a searing hell,
May spew our bones where now we dwell?

# TWO BONNETS TRIMMED WITH GREEN

We set off in the frosted over fruitless,
Morning sunshine, with jays, muttering jays,
Calling spring fever in their thoughts.
You followed me behind the engines, my windows
Misted over, but I could see you there, I
Always knew you would be there, every step of
The way, every corner, every turn in the lane.
You were always two seconds behind me,
Two unrelated items of time.

Diesel, polo's, a different world,
Out in fumed air, away from Chopin
And Rachmaninoff. The meter whizzed round
And I paid the bill. In the office a different smell,
Two little men sat there wasting time, probably
Time I'd paid for. My time. It was down to them
And their boring lives. You said you had watched me
Climb the stairs to the office and had thought that
Those legs that climbed those stairs had entwined me
Earlier. I left with you, with lapwings coloured, in
The vast, blue coloured sky.
Lapwings coloured against the trees of the forest,
Trunks like totem poles on the ridge
Of America, and the road wild and winding on.

The mansion, white, where she had lived,
Where she had laid, my mother, sweet and frail,
Where frailty failed.
It seemed odd, she no longer there. Dead and buried,
Flowers withering as all flowers must. I said my farewell
To the place with a card and a kiss for the top nurse.
A card with a cartoon of a ladybird laughing,
It was her type of card and would have made her laugh,
Then everyone would have laughed.

Two woolly hats, knitted long ago, in the
Little bungalow. Nimble fingers.
Woolly hats trimmed with green, her favourite colour.

Two woolly night hats trimmed with green, exchanged
For a smiling ladybird card, with the words
THANK YOU sprawled across the top, then with you
Again, and away from the sunlit beeches, the sunlit
Estate and the sunlit firs. Home, where the winds blow
Cold and lonely, in February, and the lapwings wheel,
And your brown eyes bathe me now the sunshine
Has gone, and I am left holding my memories and
Two little bonnets trimmed with green.

## BECKETT END

I remember Beckett End; as a boy
I spent ten happy years there from the age
Of four, in that chalk house beside the stream;
Home with the winding stairs, ten happy years.
The Beck ran coolly by from east to west,
The happy, little stream that wound its way
From its clear, bubbling spring on Rice's moor
To the white bridge where farmers' men filled up
Their carts; under the road it gurgled, out
Beyond where it became a sparkling lake,
Beyond which it joined the river Wissey.

Outside my home, across the Beck, there swayed
The Holt, the wood of many trees, the home
Of varied birds and creatures dear to me,
The memories come flooding back again
Of childhood, wood and stream and that dear place
Where I ran free in Norfolk's healthy air;
And where we fished for sticklebacks, bright red,
And romped knee-deep in summer's gold array.

## OUR TIME

Across the stars, we did not know
How our lives entwined and so
We danced that dance and it was clear
We had a life to live and share.

We found we knew the way of verse,
And marvelled at the universe
And in the fields and woods we found
The pulse of nature; all around.

We wandered far; saw mountains high,
Shimmering lakes where eagles fly
And in the midst of wonderment
We found our love and what it meant.

For my part Brenda, I must say
You've made my life one big sun-ray.
You will remain my loving friend
Until I reach my journey's end.

# THE ROLLING HILLS

How quickly have the years gone by,
How fragile now are we;
Like silken flowers out in the sun,
We near our destiny.
Down there the sparkling lakes abide
And eagles taunt the air:
We have each other to confide
And memories to share.

The rolling hills are green again,
A lark sings in the sky;
And you and I can dream again
And watch the world go by.

Was here those many years ago
We laughed our days away,
And walked the heather'd mountainsides
And glimpsed the last sun ray.
The rolling hills are out in bloom
A rainbow swathes the vale,
As hand-in-hand again we roam
Our old familiar trail.

# YOU WERE NEVER A STRANGER

You were never a stranger,
I always knew you were there;
I sensed within my being
Your so near presence somewhere.

Such a life changing moment
With you at last by my side.
Such a heart stopping feeling;
At last my life beautified.

All the heart searching longings
For someone dear to my heart.
All my wand'rings and dreamings
Led me around to the start.

Like a rainbow from glory
My life was lit up anew.
Now I walk my tomorrows'
Into the sunset with you.

## BALLAD TO AN ANGEL

The valleys are but dingy dells,
The lea a dismal hue,
The wooded hills are dreary fells
Compared, my love, to you.

My window view across the vale
Has lost its wistful pull;
The world beyond is wan and pale
But you are beautiful.

Your soft, shy eyes and tender smile,
Your grace and gentleness,
Shines far above the bitter guile
Of nature's hostile dress.

The rainbow shows a tinge of grey,
The sky no tint of blue,
The sun is but a tarnished ray
Compared, my love, to you.

The stream is harsh and weary worn,
The water meadows dull;
The singing birds seem all forlorn,
But you are beautiful.

Your lovely face and silken hair;
Such riches, I confess,
Leave nothing earthly to compare
With your sweet loveliness.

# THE WIND IS THE MESSENGER

Wind is the messenger
That blows in from the sea,
Bringing on its breezes
A message dear to me.

On the wings of the wind
I heard my true-love say,
Don't be long my darling
Before you head my way.

I'll be waiting for you,
Your footsteps in the drive,
I long to be with you,
You make me feel alive.

On the wings of the wind
I whispered my reply,
I'll be with you darling
As darkness leaves the sky.

We'll spend time together,
The time will go so fast;
I know my sweet darling
Our love will surely last.

Wind is the messenger
That blows in from the sea,
Bringing sweet messages
For you my love, and me.

## SAM'S A DOG

One night when it was windy,
And pow'r was on the blink,
Sam made a meal in twilight
Bent over his tin sink.
He ate it all with Gusto
Who was his only pet;
When morning brought the postman,
They took Sam to the vet.
Wuff, wuff!

***Chorus***
*Old Sam became a canine,*
*A canine, a canine,*
*Old Sam became a canine,*
*A great, big, yapping hound.*
*They fed him on fat turkey,*
*Fed him on fat turkey,*
*They fed him on fat turkey*
*And threw him in the pound.*
*Bootiful!*

The dog food he had eaten
When he was in the dark,
Had brought him out in black spots
And made him growl and bark.
They had a big dilemma
And wondered what to do;
Send him to the knacker's yard,
Or hand him to the zoo.
Wuff, wuff!

They sent him home with Gusto
Who took him for a walk,
And after chasing rainbows
Old Sam began to talk.
He said he felt so sorry
And he would gladly pay,
The vet remarked, in hindsight,
Each dog must have his day.
Wuff, wuff!

Sam organised a party
Each guest to bring a can.
They all felt Hale and Hearty
And cooked meat in a pan.
Hale and Hearty did not care
They saw it as a lark,
And as the party ended
They all began to bark.
Wuff,wuff!

## I SEE IN YOU

I see in you the beauty of the day,
The beauty of the morning, still and bright.
In my life you are a most precious ray
And take from me the ugly state of night.
I see you in the lark's vibrating throat,
I hear you in the waters of the sea.
You make me feel I wear the warmest coat;
Oh dearest what delights you bring to me.
I see you move with grasses and with trees.
The song you sing is like a chaffinch, free.
Your lips are like sweet kisses on the breeze,
Your strength is in your sweet simplicity.
The beauty of your sunrise is all mine,
So precious are your sinews and your wine.

# SAINT GEORGE

The red and white of England,
The flag of our Saint George;
Who never saw this country -
The land he helped to forge.

They say he slew a dragon
To save a maiden fair,
A legend in the making,
That no one can compare.

He was a Roman soldier,
Beheaded to behold,
For a faith he chose to live;
A Christian it is told.

King Richard claimed the Red Cross,
It was his battle cry,
His soldiers wore it proudly;
They were prepared to die.

Saint George our Christian martyr,
We're blessed he came our way.
So now we wear a red rose
And celebrate his day.

# MY BEAUTIFUL LOVE

My beautiful love has faded
Like the sun of an autumn day,
My beautiful love has wilted,
Has wilted and withered away.

My beautiful love was cherished
Like a very beautiful view,
It knew the spendour of sunshine
For it had the beauty of you.

My beautiful love was special
A diamond in heaven's array,
It showered me with happiness
Which never before came my way.

My beautiful love has faded
And I am so sad and forlorn,
The tears are stinging at my face
And my heart is broken and torn.

O beautiful love I need you,
Bring back to my life the sunshine,
Come back and light my world again,
Come back O sweet love and be mine.

# TIN RACING ON THE BECK

We raced those cans Reggie,
Do you remember? On the Beck.
Jam cans they were with lids removed.
Skill was required, just the right
Amount of water was needed, the right
Weight, so that the current of the
Little stream would send them
On their way at a pace,
Down from Dixon's towards the bridge.

We became expert at tin can racing
Reggie. Sometimes the stream would
Take two or three courses through
The weeds and watercress, sometimes a
Tin would become lodged in the weeds and a
Stick was required to push it free,
That was allowed; it was all in the game.
The tins were nicely coloured with
Pretty pictures of the fruit they once
Contained, and a black man's smiling face.

# THE SCARECROW AND THE BEAUTIFUL BIRD

I was a scarecrow many a year,
No soul to give me a cheery word,
No one to love and no one to care
Till I found you, my beautiful bird.

My heart was empty, just filled with straw,
When out of the blue this song I heard,
I felt a glowing not felt before
When I saw you, my beautiful bird.

I was so weary out on the hill,
All tattered and torn, looking absurd,
Lonely and cold, frustrated, until
You came along, my beautiful bird.

And now I have vowed to change my ways,
Love you forever, you have my word;
And cherish you all our golden days,
My tender, loving, beautiful bird.

## THIS GREEN PLATEAU

I overlook this green plateau
Where field-mice live and winds blow cold;
Where farmers grow row after row,
Where green turns slowly into gold;
Where field-mice gnaw the spilling grain
And skylarks sing their love refrain.

I dream beyond this greenish bliss,
This Eden fair, this green plateau.
I bless the time to reminisce,
To scheme, to strike some epic blow;
To spread some magic o'er the scene,
To keep it safe forever green.

Is now, yes now, this very day,
That this fair spot stands at its prime;
The planners could soon take away,
This lovely heritage of time
And leave it weeping, dress'd in stone,
Where I could never walk alone.

## MY DREAM AND YOU

I sought you because it was you that I sought
When dreaming, so vivid I've seen
Your beaming smile and once in awhile
I saw you so real in my dream.

I need you because it is you that I need -
The solace and comfort you bring -
The peace of mind helps me to unwind,
'Tis simply a beautiful thing.

I love you because you are mine to be loved,
So lovely, so splendid and fine,
Like burnished gold, so good to behold,
I love you because you are mine.

So now I have found you my dream springs to life,
In essence, as clear as the day -
My morning star I saw from afar
Will never again fade away.

I cherish you now like a cherry in bloom
Whose blossoms are joyful like you,
A cherry fair, with much loving care
Who turns all my grey skies to blue.

So now my sweet darling the world is all ours,
Come hold me and kiss me my love.
Our joy shall be for eternity,
As bright as the stars up above.

# MY ENGLAND

Burn with love my England
This world has need of thee;
Deep within life's ocean,
You burn triumphantly.

Your valleys sing with love,
Your mountains ring with joy;
For you are the strong one
No tyrant can destroy.

Your word is your motto,
Your language is their tongue;
You praise the Creator
And let His songs be sung.

Like the cliffs of Dover
That stretch up from the shore;
You are true and mighty,
The England I adore.

Out there like a beacon
You shine with all your might;
Such a bright example
Above the bitter night.

Burn with love my England
For you are just and free;
Fly the flag of freedom
Across life's hostile sea.

# ONE MORNING

I woke up one morning,
The sun in the sky.
I thought, what a good day
To see the world by.

I saddled my pony
And off I did go,
Beyond the green meadow
Where winds softly blow.

To seek my fair maiden,
To ask for her hand;
Is all that I dreamt of
Beyond this good land.

I heard her voice calling
In valley and stream,
And saw her feet dancing
On ev'ry sunbeam.

Amid the grey mountains
I there pitched my tent.
I had not one penny
To pay a night's rent.

At last by the river
I came to her door,
And found she had married
The morning before.

She told me she loved me
But it was too late,
She said she had waited
Alone at her gate.

Until one fine morning
Amid sparkling dew
A farmer came calling
And said he'd be true.

So with my heart broken
We said our goodbyes,
She blew me some kisses
With tears in her eyes.

I found myself riding
Towards the sunset
A day to remember
A day to forget.

His face was familiar
The man she had wed,
And then I remembered,
His wife was not dead.

I turned around quickly
And back I did go,
Beyond the green meadow
Where winds softly blow.

I saw the dawn breaking
A veil of the night,
It was my intention
To tell of her plight.

Back there at the cottage
I found she had gone,
Gone, gone with the farmer
On their honeymoon.

My spirits were sagging,
I wanted to die.
To find my sweet woman
I knew I must try.

Amid the grey mountains
I rested a while,
And dreamt of her beauty
And cursed at his guile.

I heard her voice calling
Like wind on the sea,
I thought of the morrow
Of setting her free.

At last near a farmstead,
I found their abode
I told her the story
Surrounding the rogue.

We fought in the farm yard,
My rival and I,
And I was the victor,
He fell with a cry.

We rode off together
To each take a vow,
Beyond the green meadows
Where winds softly blow.-

And now we are happy,
So happy and free.
We watch the sun setting
My sweetheart and me.

# I BREATHE YOU IN

I breathe you in, you are my air,
You are my way, my step, my stair;
Just as the sea breathes in the tide,
I breathe you in to stay alive.

Without your eyes I could not see.
Without my sight I'd fade and die,
Without your love I'd not survive,
I breathe you in to stay alive.

The trees breathe in the mighty sun,
So do the flow'rs, yes everyone.
They need the bees, bees need a hive,
And I need you to stay alive.

Without your smile I could not be,
Nor would I have a destiny.
You give to me the will to strive,
And I need you to stay alive.

The earth breathes in the humble rain,
I breathe you in to live again.
And on your breath, I simply thrive,
I breathe you in to stay alive.

Just as the day breathes in the light,
I breathe you in with all my might.
My inner calm you did contrive,
I breathe you in to stay alive.

# THE SOUND OF FREEDOM

I heard the sound of freedom
As I crossed the heathered moor,
I saw a rainbow coming,
Blessed be the poor.

I heard the sound of freedom
In the song of ev'ry lark.
I heard the joyful voices
Singing in the dark.

I heard the sound of freedom
As I'd never heard before.
All the sorrowing had gone
With the bloody war.

She stood there waiting for me
As I walked along the street.
The bells peeled out the freedom
Amid the ribbons, neat.

We hugged a hug of freedom,
Re-united at long last,
Our dreams spread out before us,
Gone the warring blast.

# IT'S A LOVELY NIGHT

It's a lovely night for loving
If only I were with you,
With the stars up above
We could make love,
Make love the whole night through.

It's a lovely night for sharing,
Sharing the joys that we have;
We have plenty to share,
No need to care,
We have each others' love.

It's a lovely night for wishing,
Wishing that you were with me.
Only one little kiss
Is all I wish,
It would be heavenly.

It's a lovely night for dreaming,
Dreaming of times that have gone.
I have nothing to do
But dream of you,
All on my very own.

It's a lovely night for hoping,
Hoping to see you so clear,
And I don't feel so sad,
Hope makes me glad,
And I am filled with cheer.

# I WILL NEVER KNOW YOU WELL

I will never know you well
For you are like the seasons of the world,
The shifting sands, the springs,
The varied songs of birds.

I will never hear you well
For your voice rings like the rain,
Like the flutes of unseen players,
Not of one tone or tune.

I will never see you well
For you are so changeable,
So many shapes and colours,
Sometimes I see you like a tree standing firm,
And then I look again and you are gone,
Or moving in the mist away from me,
And I can't stop you going from my view.

Sometimes I feel you are like a book
I have read so many times
And know so well,
And yet when I reach out for its pages
They are new to me;
Not one word I find familiar,
Not one passage old or worn,
But new, refreshing, mystic, precious,
Each chapter, sentence and each word.

# MY BLOOM SO SWEET AND RARE

Cloudy days have long since gone
And gone the winter, bare.
Hours of lonely solitude
And moments of despair,
Melted now, gone with the dew,
By a bloom so sweet and rare.

All around, above, below
Were briars to rip and tear
And within my weary soul
Were moments of despair,
Joy springs in my heart again
Through a bloom so sweet and rare.

Magic in the sweetest face
Leaves nothing to compare;
Here within my outstretched arms,
The answer to my prayer,
I love you so, this you know,
My flower so sweet and rare.

## GOOD-NIGHT MY ANGEL

Good-night my angel may you sleep
Where devils dare not tread.
May the sun be always shining
About your sleepy head.

Farewell my angel may you rest
Where fair winds always blow.
May you arise in paradise
Where sweetest rivers flow.

I will so miss your fleeting steps,
Miss your laughing cry.
Oh I will miss you all my days,
Why did you have to die.

I loved the many hours we spent
Together on the heath,
For we were very happy then
But now you rest beneath.

I needed you as I grew old,
Much more than you will know;
But life has swung its pendulum
And I am lonely now.

Good-night my lovely sleeping doll,
You were my golden ray.
I thank my stars for knowing you,
I thank them ev'ry day.

# ALL THE CONFIDENCE

All the confidence I had
Has been drained from me.
Like the mist drains from the moor.
All the love I had
Has been lost, is gone
Like leaves fetched to the
Four corners of the earth
By the laughing wind.

All the tears I had
Have been shed, they
Have rolled away.
Bee's eyes can see
A better day than I.
The slit of life consumes
Me like a fold in a blanket
Consumes a feather, lost and
Faded, defied and of no
Consequence.

# THIS IS MY NATIVE LAND

This is my native land
The land I love the best.
On her green fields I stand
Where my ancestors rest.

This is my native sea
Where armies went to war
And kinsfolk fought for me
Beyond this blessed shore.

This is my native sky
Where flies no hostile foe,
I watch her clouds drift by
As winds of freedom blow.

This is my native lair
Where all can play a part,
A multicoloured sphere
Where beats the human heart.

A country come of age
With still great works to do,
A nationhood on stage
Where dreams can yet come true.

# FEELING FREE

I like to spend a quiet day
When the neighbours are away;
It's peaceful then and quite serene,
No sound of noisy grass machine:
There's just the wind and me.

My garden seems a private place
Where I can stroll at my own pace;
Take things easy or reminisce,
For it's a sort of short-lived bliss.
My inner self and me.

But when the neighbours return home
My garden fills again with gloom;
Their noise upsets my train of thought,
And ends abruptly my rare sport
Of just a feeling free.

## ONE MORE SUMMER

Just one more summer, Brenda
To watch the woods grow green.
To hear the ancient cuckoo,
See swallows o'er the stream.
Just one more summer, Brenda,
To dance the nights away;
Watch the full moon roam the sky
In its emphatic way.
Just one more summer, Brenda,
To hear the curlew's call,
Amid the grassy meadows,
Before the snowflakes fall.

# IVY

Ivy is eighty, unable to see
Dew in the morning or leaf on the tree.
Images liveth within her mind's eye
Of children's faces and blues of the sky.
Clear memories dear, replaces her sight,
Gardens of roses appear in her night.
Glazing concealing her vision'ry spark
Leaves her daydreaming alone in the dark.

Skill of the surgeon and colours anew,
Unshackled her vision; eyes again true.
Ivy is ninety and able to see
Gold in the meadow, the sycamore-tree,
Children's bright faces, all heaven alight,
And gardens of roses, red, pink and white.

# NOW THE MAY IS ON THE BOUGH

Now the may is on the bough
And breeze light as a feather;
I recall my solemn vow
To love, my love, forever.
I recall the day we met,
The day I met my treasure,
And I have not one regret
To love, my love, forever.

Blossoms lovely as her eyes
Ran rampant o'er the hedges,
Fluffy clouds hung in the skies
And birds sang from the sedges.
Years have trundled on and by
With heartbreak and with pleasure;
I will love her 'till I die,
Forever, and forever.

Balmy as the days of May;
When strolling at our leisure,
We rejoice in ev'ry way
Our many years together.
Now the may is on the bough
And fair the May-time weather,
I affirm my solemn vow
To love, my love, forever.

## SHE WALKED INTO THE GARDEN

She walked into the garden
Where roses sip the dew,
She walked into the garden
In her vain search for you;
And on her feet were blue shoes,
Her dress was also blue,
She walked into the garden
In her vain search for you.

Her eyes were wet with crying,
The tears rolled down her face;
And there is no denying
She beautified that place.
Her steps were far from certain,
Her mission not in doubt,
She came into the garden
So she could seek you out.

I told her you were absent
But had not seen you go,
She sat beneath the porch way
And seemed not what to do.
She then rose up and left me
Across the sunlit lawn,
I knew not what to tell her
Except that you had gone.

## OUT OF THE MIST

Out of the mist came a black man,
Out of the lash of the whip
Into the glare of a nightmare -
Sure hands to steady the ship.

Out of the mist came a leader
Out of the African sun,
To bring hope to all the people -
A new era had begun.

Out of the mist came Obama
His mission ever so clear;
To rid the world of tyranny
For the things that we hold dear.

# THE STORYTELLER

I met a man the other day,
He is a storyteller.
He tells of wild deer at their play,
And snowy lanes in winter.

He is a very kindly man,
A man who loves to chatter,
He writes about the things he can,
About the things that matter.

He said he needed not a lot,
Just health and wit and seeing,
He said he worried not a jot -
He is a humble being.

He raised his hand and pointed to
A jet plane flying over,
A skylark singing in the blue,
And purple fields of clover.

Ah, there you have inventiveness,
Of music and of colour,
These are the things that I address,
When scribbling in my parlour.

I met a man the other day,
He is a storyteller,
And of him I can truely say
He is a quaint, old fellah.

## TO MY MOTHER

Age creeps across her features
Like that wispy season autumn,
Which spreads change and decay
On valley, field and hill.

Age wrinkles her as autumn
Wrinkles them, yet her beauty
Shines through still.

In her eyes there beams a
Childish wonder; from her lips
There blows a kiss of love.

She has worked hard her long
Life over, lived Godly well and
Hurt nor feared no man.

The russet tones that scamper
With the autumn chill.
Do not grip her will.

Her faith is strong enough
To see her through the
Darkest nights that there
Could ever be to an eternal spring
Where not one flower will die
Nor one weed mar her view.

Her measured gait has not the strength
It once enjoyed, when years gone by,
She walked with her two sons the
Oak leafed lanes, and taught them life
And what life means.

Her hearing too is now below its
Youthful best, but still awake enough
To hear a robin's dreams.

All through her long, hard life,
Her body, mind and spirit have
Been free.

Now in high autumn she suffers
Not one self-appointed ill to
Weigh her down.

She truly is a happy soul
And cheerful too, with a
Kindly word for all who drift her way.

They that know her, respect her,
For she is wiser than the most of them.

Her heart is young, her spirit
Long decided. She moulded well,
Her well of wisdom, when clay was young,
Now from its deep rejoicing depths,
She drinks a water fresher than the
Flowers of spring.

## SILENT NOW

Distant now the very noise
Distant and forlorn;
Distant too, the river sounds
And the waving corn.

Duller now than yellow now,
Duller now than red;
Duller now and mellow now
Are the things she said.

Faded now her avid smile,
And her eyes of blue.
Faded too her soft white skin
Faded from my view.

Greener now the very place,
Lower too the hill,
Faded now the flow'ry wreath,
Silent now and still.

# RHUBARB

One day when I was feeling glum
I went to see my dear, old mum.
She said. 'You are a silly child'
Why can't you be like others - Wild?'
So thereupon I climbed a tree
And shouted loudly. 'Wee! Wee! Wee!'

One night when I was feeling sad
I paid a call on my poor dad.
He said to me. 'You silly son,
Take up a sport, learn how to run.'
I boiled some rhubarb in a pot,
And gulped it down, the bloomin' lot.
Day and night for a week or more
I ran like heck from door to door.

Now I have reached maturity
And know at last what's good for me:
No longer do I seek advice,
I solve my problems in a trice;
And now and then I climb a tree
And from a branch shout. 'WEE! WEE! WEE!'

## THE OTHER YOU

He pointed to the sunrise;
A lark sang up above,
And somewhere in the greenwood
I heard a turtle dove.

I'm down the pubs all evening
And chase the tote each day.
I watch a lot of football
The rest I cannot say.

He plucked a knapweed seed head
And put it to his jaw
And played a little ditty
I'd never heard before.

We stumbled on a red fox
And harebells on the hill,
And then to my amazement
A wren began to trill.

I stayed abroad this evening,
The moon hung big and bright
And on a frosted gorse bush,
A spider spun all night.

I stroll old nature's byways,
Each glance a diff'rent view;
Oh, have you seen: may I ask,
The other side of you?

# CRIMSON DREAM

I gazed upon an oak-tree
Which swayed beside a brook,
And there a crimson lady
Read from a magic book.

And when the clouds of mist rose
Above the waters cool,
I noticed her reflection
A dancing in the pool.

Her image was so ugly
Amid the crimson lace,
Her little book resembled
A frog without a face.

And I became enchanted
Like some deluded fool
And when she called me over
I joined her by the pool.

The solitary oak-tree
Was filled with bells so small,
A bluebird sang so sweetly
Without a care at all.

The crimson lady's beauty
Just gripped me like a spell
She pointed to the oak-tree
And then the bluebird fell.

She told me that she loved me
For loves unselfish sake.
I turned my head to kiss her
And found myself awake.

## NO MORE THAN A WHISPER

Yes, elegant! One of mystery,
Gentle no doubt of hand and lips,
Albeit out of my reach.

Formidable I fear, and so true.
Inadequate am I with no
Right to reach out to you.

No right to effect your attention
Let alone your love.

I could never reach you,
Even if by some miracle I managed to,
I would fall once more beneath your gaze.

I could not live in such a hapless state
For long, knowing you had the edge
I would bore you sooner than later;
I could not fuel a sham forever.

You, with your small hands and big I.Q.
Oh yes, you use your brain gently,
It barely ticks over to keep up with me,
Me and my flickering wit.

Be, my love, a whisper in my ear,
No more than a gentle breeze;
I would burn up and become as nothing
If you really stepped into my world.

# THE DREAM

Your face seems familiar,
Have I seen you before?
Perhaps in a dream once
You came through my door.

We walked through my dream-land
To the source of my dream,
I wanted to sleep on,
You're part of my scheme.

I remember those eyes
So alive in the night;
Your clothes are familiar
All tinted with white.

You gave me some shelter,
And the clothes that I wear
Were by your hands fashioned
With infinite care.

Your face is familiar,
I have seen it before;
I've dreamt of you often,
At least times a score.

Perhaps in a dream once
At the end of life's race,
I cried out for mercy
And there saw your face.

# THE HOODED MAN

The hooded man hung in the lane
As darkness fell to night,
Above his hood the Scots pines stood
And knew not black from white.

He walked beneath their burdened boughs
And there paced up and down,
Dark shadows fell around his head
Around his hooded gown.

At times he stopped and paused for thought,
At times he shook his head;
The wind did cry in Scots pine tops
A whining from the dead.

Then in a moment of the moon
His face stood from the dark,
His lips were moving but no word
Did he in fact remark.

And then again the moon did burn
Like sun upon a wave;
The hooded figure fell and knelt
Beside a tiny grave.

The church was grey, an awesome grey,
Its spire a sombre tone.
The hooded figure stood upright
And then began to moan.

Then suddenly there rose a cry
And through the shadows came,
A woman with a lighted torch
And she did call his name.

# DON'T LET THE MOMENT GO

Don't let the moment go
Like sand through our fingers.
That's all we need to know.
Don't let the moment go.

Don't let the moment go
Like a cry in the wind;
Just let the moment flow,
Don't let the moment go.

Don't let the moment go
Like the sun at nightfall,
We are together now,
Don't let the moment go.

Don't let the moment go
Like dew in the morning;
Now that our love will grow,
Don't let the moment go.

Don't let the moment go,
Lets grow the seeds we sow.
We have it all us two,
Don't let the moment go.

# BEAUTIFUL AND FREE

Dad said mother was beautiful,
Just like a summer tree;
He told me she was beautiful,
So beautiful was she.

He told me that she passed away
When I was only three
And she was very beautiful,
Just like an autumn tree.

He had a photograph of her
And once he let me see.
I saw that she was beautiful,
So beautiful was she.

Her letters to my father dear,
Were wonderful to read,
She was so very beautiful,
So beautiful indeed.

And just before the old man died,
He softly said to me;
You are so very beautiful,
As beautiful as she.

Now when I see a summer wood
Or view an autumn tree;
I think of him and think of her,
So beautiful and free.

# MY SWEET PRINCESS

You surely are my precious love,
The sweetest love in this fair land.
You truly are my sweet princess
And how I long to hold your hand.

I long to run my fingers through
Your silken hair, so good to see.
I long to touch your face so much,
I long to hold you close to me,

Your tender eyes are softer than
The shadows of my troubled night,
And yet your eyes lift up my life
And fill my world with light so bright.

Your loving smile is fresher than
The morning dew that clothes the hill,
And yet your smile, your loving smile
Fades not away but shines on still.

I long to kiss your wondrous lips
A thousand times, O can you tell?
I want to press them close to mine,
So take me from this living hell.

The way you walk delights me so,
No princess walks with surer poise,
I crave to walk alongside you,
To happiness 'neath brighter skies.

# FOR BRENDA

Flower of the meadow
Bloom year upon year;
There's no one, sweet flower
Like you to compare.

Rest on my bosom
And dance on the hill,
When you are sleeping
I'll think of you still.

When I am dreaming
I see you so well,
Flower of the meadow
I simply can tell -

You are the finest
In heart and in soul
I would be lonely
If I walked alone.

When the wind's blowing
You gently sway too;
Only look backwards
A moment or two.

Since our chance meeting,
You grow in my heart,
Flower of the meadow
We never should part.

# DIANA

Those loving eyes: sweet mother's eyes
That saw her two boys grow
Can no longer visualise
The sorrow that they know.
The world had watched her ev'ry move,
Had seen her laugh and cry,
And now they come with heartfelt love,
To say their last goodbye.

We bring you blossoms from the heart;
The mourners seem to say,
You brought us love right from the start
In your own precious way.
The lame, the dying, those in need,
You took each cross to bear;
You gave them joy as was your creed
When they were in despair.

The world at large will act upon
Your plea to banish tears.
Your wondrous spirit will live on
Through future's untold years.
Our dear, bright light, our shining star
Has faded from our view.
You were the brightest star by far
Sick children ever knew.

## LIKE A BIRD

Like a bird, you have flown, far away,
O so high, 'cross the sea, through the sky;
Here I wait patiently 'till the day
You return, safe and sound, by and by.

We are friends, only friends, yet I know
There's a glow in our hearts like a flame,
And as time journeys on it could grow
And consume, like a flame, all our pain.

We can bare, be sincere, in our cares,
We can share, if we dare, all our joys;
We can wear happiness through the years,
Like a bird, we can reach, for the skies.

Love can flow, this we know, like a brook,
Love can be, we agree, O so frail,
Time will tell, if the spell from life's book
Can be more than a mere fairytale.

I can wait, contemplate, by and by
For the day you return, O my word!
Like a bird, you will fly through the sky,
Back again, O my word, like a bird.

# BEYOND THIS PRECIOUS MOMENT

Beyond this precious moment,
So feeble as I am,
I just want to hold you
And reach you if I can.

As with so many daydreams
That fade before the eye,
I am scared this vision
Is bound, alas, to die.

I want to share forever
Your smile, your tender touch.
For I know I'm falling
In love with you so much.

You make me feel so lucky,
You make me feel so proud
Yet you are a stranger
Amid the milling crowd.

I hope to see the sunsets
Light up your lovely face,
There is no denying
You fill my world with grace.

I step into the future
So anxious and so keen,
To become enchanted
And bring to life this dream.

# BROKEN GLASS

My dreams are beyond repair,
Just like broken glass I fear;
Images are clouded now,
Splintered is my mind of woe.

Broken glass is all I see;
Fragments of myself in me.
Breaking glass is all I hear,
Cutting deep in my despair.

In my dreams I hear the sound
Of glass breaking all around;
Visions which were once so clear
Now seem doomed to disappear.

Once her face was in the glass,
Now I see it's gone, alas.
Once her smile was radiant,
Now I see a smile that's spent.

If I could but look anew,
See glass sparkle like the dew;
If I could but shift the cloud,
I would see her bright and proud.

I'm left now with reflections,
Impossible to surpass,
Pitted with imperfections
Like the panes of broken glass.

# THE PRICE OF LOVE

Is this the price we have to pay?
Is this the price of love?
All our dreams seem far away,
Like the skies above.

But love is bright and beautiful,
Just like a summer's day;
Love is real and wonderful,
Sweeter than the may.

We count the ships that come and go
Across the mighty sea;
Count the tides that ebb and flow
Through eternity.

So in my arms I hold you tight
And look into your eyes,
As the moon lights up the night
Stars wake in the skies.

And in our hearts new love is born,
Hope dispels our fears.
Love shines through the bitter storm;
Wipes away our tears.

# AT HEAVEN'S DOOR

One day when I was all alone
I knocked at Heaven's door
And there within I found my love,
An angel to adore.

On her bright face there beamed a smile,
Our eyes met instantly,
We fell in love, my dove, my love;
How happy we will be.

We walk towards a rainbow new
My angel love and I,
And we have found our pot of gold
Beneath a tender sky.

I had to go to Heaven's gate
To find my sweet romance,
Because upon this squalid earth
I did not have a chance.

An angel from the realms above,
She is without a doubt,
And I will dearly love her now
Until my days run out.

For if I ever let her down
I'll lose her that's for sure,
She will return to paradise
And leave me to endure.

# YOU ARE MY PRECIOUS MOMENTS

I miss you dearly when you are away;
I cannot rest, I ache so much for you.
You are the precious moments of my day,
You are my rainbows' ever tender hue.
Sometimes you seem a mirage in a dream,
Somehow you drift like mist across a beach;
Just like a ghost, an image in a stream,
Like an illusion, so far out of reach.
But when at last we meet once in a while
The womanhood in you is real indeed;
You have a grace, an energizing style
That satisfies my longings ev'ry need.
You are so fine, so fair in majesty;
You mean the whole wide world and more to me.

# THE CAST AWAY JAR

In a cast away jar
I found you mirrored
In the glass.
All around the dew wept
Tears in the grass.

The yellow sun melted the dew,
It did not destroy the image of you
In the glass.

The meadow sang,
Pollen floated lazily by.
At the rim of the hill
I had to stand still,
As I thought I heard you cry.

The cast away jar
Was all on its own,
Your mirrored face
Had somehow gone.

The flowers held their heads
As if in pain;
Oh how I wish I could see you again.

The cast away jar moaned in the wind,
Like a dead echo;
There was nothing left for me.
I had to go.

# SONG

I have no right
To pry into your thinking,
Or look into your pretty, little head,
I have no claim
To know what you are dreaming
When in your bath or tucked up in your bed.

It's not that I
Don't long to share your secrets
Or ache to hold you gently in my arms;
It's not that I
Don't want to share your kisses
Or be enriched by your endearing charms.

I'd like to know exactly what you're dreaming
And wonder if you see me in your dreams,
I'd like to know
Exactly what you're scheming
And if I count among your many schemes.

There is no rush,
No need for you to hurry,
Do not trouble your pretty little head,
For I can wait
Until, my love, you're ready;
O I can wait and dream of you instead.

The day will come
When you will be beside me
And whisper words so tenderly I know,
So I can wait
Until that day approaches,
And from that day our love will surely grow.

# WELL OF LOVE

I have a well of love for you,
Forever deep, forever true;
In my heart you will always be,
My shining star, my destiny.

You are my ever shining star;
My sweetest love is what you are,
And I will never walk alone,
As long as you will be my own.

You are the essence of my joy,
You are the love that I live by;
And in your eyes are valleys green,
Within their midst I am serene.

And in your face is hope for me,
It radiates with charity;
And in your smile is happiness,
My heart is fill'd with joyful bliss.

You are my very special love,
My angel from the realms above;
I feel like paradise is near,
As in my arms I hold you dear.

I have a well of love for you,
Forever fresh, forever new,
In my life you will always be,
A rising, shining star to me.

# WOMAN

Nature has a way with us,
She formulates our dreams;
Has no room for cosiness
However hard it seems.

Nature is the vehicle
Which drives the world along;
Roaring seas and earthquakes
Mid roses and bird song.

She is unpredictable
Like a woman, in her ways,
Times of gracious fortitude
Are mixed with anxious days.

Nature has an empathy
With womanhood and thus,
She gives birth to all around
And woman all of us.

# FASHIONED

Nature fashioned you so well,
Conjured up a special spell;
Engineered with diamonds fine
All the beauty that is thine.

Your persona shines afar.
Casting light where'er you are;
Spreading joy to all you know:
This is why I love you so!

# THE CELLAR BAR

We met in the cellar bar,
Mid music and soft lights,
We danced in the cellar bar
The first of many nights.

The mellow walls around us
Echoed a mood of love,
The cellar bar that found us
Was manna from above.

Her bearing was exquisite
And gentle was her smile,
When in my arms I held her
'Twas heaven for awhile.

I thought her shy and happy,
We danced to each refrain.
The quick ones and the slow ones -
Shear pleasure to my brain.

So soon the night was over,
The magic played no more.
Hand-in-hand we walked away
From that old cellar floor.

The night was one of wonder,
For I had found a star;
O, I had found a sweetheart
In that old cellar bar.

## THE FISHERMAN

Solitude is without price,
Life a gamble like a dice;
Man and rod and man and boat
All alone, alone, remote.
Time to think, forget the race
There amid the realms of space.
Shadows fall as prey slide by
In the dim light of the sky.
Fragile there and in deep thought
Thinking if his prey is caught,
Will it die or be set free,
Will he feast on fish for tea?

# LONELINESS

When I see the birds fly
In flocks across the sky,
I know that summer's waning
And winter's drawing nigh.

When I hear the bells toll
From yonder spire of stone,
I know that I'll be spending
The long, dark nights alone.

Now the leaves are falling
So gently on the breeze,
And in my mind I see her,
Just skipping through the trees.

Then the sad truth hits me
And taunts me like a spell,
For she has gone like childhood
Into the deepest well.

Mist engulfs the waters,
But still her cries are clear;
And they will haunt forever
And fill me with despair.

Lonely is the winter
It's loneliness I dread,
Young birds are raised in springtime,
But sadly not the dead.

# BUS RIDE

Horses dreaming, running races,
Gardens growing nurtured crops,
Partridges in coveys squatting,
Children waiting at bus stops.
Hedges flying, faster, faster,
Lapwings winging with the sun.
Drivers wait at country junctions;
For the young ones it is fun.

Tractor's ploughing ever straighter,
Fill the sky with seagulls' calls,
People chatter, money rattle,
Cash to spend at market stalls.
On a corner waits a woman,
Scarf on head and bag in hand,
Clatter, chatter, always chatter,
Through the mellow pasture-land.

Rooks in flocks, black as a bad dream,
Weave and turn and filch the soil.
Hamlets go by many-coloured,
Passengers snooze for a while;
In the vista lies the township,
In my bones there runs the sound;
Round the corner waits the friendship,
Pilgrims who are market bound.

# SHADES OF LIFE

We, all the world over, love, laugh and cry:
We all live and love and then we all die.
The stars in the sky all fall in despair,
So why should we worry? Why should we care?
The hungry crave for their next crust of bread;
Some of us wander in search of our dead,
Life can be cruel, like the cruel sea,
Some humans are caged whilst others are free.
Hist'ry repeats itself, we never learn,
Some nations look on as others just burn.
Our lives are a maze of myst'ry and woe;
It is hard to distinguish friend from foe,
And yet there is light amid all the shade,
And a perspective in what has been made.

## TOOTHLESS TIGER
*(A Country Music Song)*


You had an iron grip on me,
You seemed so strong and wise;
I trusted you as women do
But you were in disguise.
And you fooled me into thinking
That you were right for me,
But at each turn, you let me down,
And brought me misery.

*Chorus*
*You're simply a toothless tiger,*
*A tiger without fight,*
*A typical toothless tiger,*
*You snarl but have no bite.*
*You're worse than any alley cat*
*An alley ever saw,*
*A whimpering toothless tiger,*
*I'm showing you the door.*

You rant and rave and carry on,
You promised me the moon.
You said you would take care of me,
But you are a buffoon,
I never should have trusted you,
It was a big mistake.
It's over now, get out of here,
You're nothing but a fake.

## MOST BEAUTIFUL

There never was more beautiful
A tiger or a whale,
A rainbow or a mountain top,
A river or a vale.
There never was more beautiful,
More beautiful or true,
No thing within this splendid world
More beautiful than you.

You have a personality
So mystical and fine.
You have a certain quality
So rare and so divine.
Your eyes are tender, loving eyes,
Your hair spun from star rays,
You are, my dear, so beautiful
In many differ'nt ways.

There never was more beautiful
A sunset or sunrise,
A lily or a daffodil,
The oceans or the skies.
There never was more beautiful,
More beautiful or true,
No thing within this precious world,
More beautiful than you.

## MAN'S DREAM

O how they shimmer so brightly,
Grasses so tall in the sun;
O how they sway, this way, that way,
Taking the wind for a run.

Like dreams and desires of mankind
So bright in shadowy fear;
They come and they go, to and fro,
Sharing both care and despair.

See how the tall trees stretch upwards,
Pointing so high to the sky;
So dark and stark in deep shadow,
Blown in the wind like a toy.

Man sets his stall on a mountain,
Then sinks in quick sands below;
One moment he's like a fountain
And then has no place to go.

The grasses will seed forever,
The trees will feed from the dew,
But man will be lost forever
Unless he dreams something new.

# THE WHITE OWL

The white owl flew o'er the churchyard,
Low above the graves of old;
Silent as the dead it pondered
Over sinews long since cold.
Ivy on the church spire trembled,
Shadows by the score crept in;
In the faintness of the darkness
There seemed clawing fingers, thin.

Was that an eye in the shadows?
Or just a cat on the wall
Or a rat, a bat or church mouse
Amid the wind and owl's call?
Is there someone in the porch way?
The wind is moaning in pain.
The owl stretches on a tombstone
Then flies to the belfry again.

The white owl peered from the belfry
Over the living and dead;
The wind scratched the walls with ivy,
And never a word was said.
The moon hurled the clouds asunder,
The graves shone up ghostly white
And there walked a lonely bridegroom
Out in the dead of the night.

# SHADOWS

The lane falls deep to silentness;
I cannot visualise her dress.
Her face has vanished with the day
And has desire to stay that way.
I know not where the wind has gone,
And clouds have locked away the moon.

Within my heart, within this calm
I fear some awful thing may harm
Me as I stand here not at ease;
If only blew a better breeze
To calm my fear and my despair,
I would away without a care.

And fall beneath a changing scene
Where I could sink into a dream,
And hold her tightly at my side,
And never more from me would hide
Her pretty eyes, her loving smile;
Oh if I could but dream awhile.

But if I slept my dream would be
Not such a happy one for me;
My heart would ache, my bones would too
And so my wretchedness would grow.
So better now I must confess,
That shadows hide away her dress.

# AT WINTER'S EDGE

At winter's edge, it seemed the spring
Would lack its fine romance,
I knew not then, the reckoning
Of your redeeming glance.
At winter's edge, my mind was set
On loneliness outright;
The nightingale I would forget
And dragonflies in flight.

I was then jolted from this spell
By your surpassing smile,
The cold and rain did not dispel
My feelings, nor defile;
And now the sap pumps through each vein
With vigour like the spring,
For me the world is fine again;
The nightingale doth sing.

# YOU

When you wave across the room
And smile the way you do,
You take away the gloom
And the loneliness I knew;
My empty heart is fill'd with
A rare and lovely song,
And this I do remember
Although the nights are long.

When you dance across the floor
And smile the way you do,
You open up the door
Of a garden I once knew;
The sun shone all the day there,
The sky was always blue
And in it I was happy
Like when I dance with you.

When you whisper in my ear
And smile the way you do,
I pause that I may hear
Your sweet sentiments so true;
When you laugh and tilt your head
Your hair shines in the light,
Then I think of you instead
Of cursing my cold night.

Not one kiss can pass our lips
For we are only friends,
We just touch finger-tips
As the last dance fades and ends;
When it's time to say goodbye
And time has seen us through,
Then you wave across the room
And smile the way you do.

# QUESTIONS

So where does truth abide,
Where does tolerance reign.
Where is hope this Christmastide,
What had terror to gain?

Here the vision is blurred,
What is right, what is wrong,
Yet this is not so absurd;
Each creed mouths its own song.

Truth is the ghost at hand,
A phantom to the ear;
Hope a hobo 'bout the land,
Juggling both joy and fear.

So dogma should be caged
And tolerance set free.
Let the nation's war be waged
To fight for harmony.

# CANDLES

Candles adorn the Christmas tree,
Bring to the home a warm glow;
Candles sparkle, shine and shimmer
Like the sun on newborn snow.
Candles glimmer and they twinkle
Like the star of Bethlehem,
Candles burn in ev'ry nation,
Melt the coldest hearts of men.

I will light a Christmas candle
For the loved ones I have known,
One for Mother, one for Father,
One for the love that has grown.
Light a candle for the children
Caught up in the wrath of war;
Light a candle for all people,
For the hungry and the poor.

I will light an Advent candle
On a wreath along an aisle,
I will cherish peace at Christmas
And be still, just for awhile.
Candles tremble and they falter
Like the lives of you and I,
In a moment, unsuspected,
Candles flicker, fade and die.

# THIS CHRISTMAS

This Christmas time we celebrate
Our cosmopolitan estate,
No more the blackened windows shroud
The Nazi bombers from the crowd.

For we are broke from tyranny
And lift our hearts with proud degree.
We celebrate in this new age
Each teenage youth, each scholar, - sage.

For heroes most have paid the price,
They were there then when fell the dice;
Of youth today, they care? Do they?
They think not much how come they play.

It's left to us, the moulded sort,
To teach them all why brave men fought,
And why the city shines once more
When once was brutalised by war.

In this green land we celebrate
With turkey piled upon the plate,
And carols 'round the Christmas tree;
Our heads held high, for we are free.

# GETTING HETTIE

We went for some Christmas cheer,
Assignment in the night,
Moon all hazy, trees all bare,
A mission to delight.

Purring felines everywhere,
Each one with its own charm.
Hettie showed no sign of fear,
Nor would she come to harm.

Mother, blind, her eyes so bright,
A smile dawns on her face;
The little cat, black as night
Has found a wondrous place.

Friends they are and happy too,
Long may they be content;
Each for each the long days through,
Love shared and truly meant.

# LAST WORDS

You are the morning,
A life that is dawning;
You are a flower
That's waiting to bloom.

I am at midnight,
With no morning in sight,
An old warrior
With no strength to roam.

You are the morning,
And the spring of a stream,
You have a lifetime
To laugh and to dream.

I am at midnight
And my stream's nearly dry,
My wandering thoughts
Are ready to die.

You are the morning
A star just arising;
You are all ready
To burst into day.

I am at midnight
Going is my own light;
You are just dawning
As I fade away.

# ALL ACROSS

All across the day I wandered
Where the wind fell from the air;
All across the night I slumbered,
Never sleeping anywhere.

All across the world I wandered
Where the sun fell from the trees.
All the time I paused and pondered:
Were there greater worlds than these?

In a world where time is counted,
Over which the rocks lie strewn;
I did wonder where the haunted
Sleep beneath the weary moon.

I did rest on moonlit hillside;
Heard the water rushing down,
I did walk at ev'ry dawning
Not to find a silken gown.

# MEN IN A BUBBLE

Old men and young men
All in a bubble,
Bouncing along in
The wind of the world.

Faces all twisted,
Eyes ever misted;
Unable to see
The rim of the sun.

Dizzy with bouncing
Over and over,
All going nowhere
At a great pace.

Illusions repeated,
Lives long defeated,
Disfigured they bounce
In their bubble of space.

Their colours not clear,
They bounce anyway,
Not able to see
The night from the day.

Old men and young men,
All drifting along.
They bounce in confusion
And sing their sick song.

# A TURNING WORLD

The human soul is the human cry,
The inner state is evil or joy,
The wholesome earth its oceans and sky,
Things of beauty to the human eye,
The forces of evil shan't destroy.

To erode the things we cherish dear,
To shadow the sun with dreaded fear,
Mangle the flesh and cripple the air,
And trample our freedoms with despair,
Are motions for sure we cannot bear.

To restore our dreams from endless blight,
To manage our world with tireless might,
To ravage our fears from awful plight,
To enjoy a peace for our delight,
Are within the grasp of forceful sight.

# NATURAL
# WORLD

# WINTER SNIPE

The winter snipe is forced to go,
Battered by the driven snow,
Beyond his home, his marshy flow;
Beaten by the winds that blow.
The sallow meres are frozen o'er;
Ice-bound fast, the rigid moor:
His reedy homeland, bitter, raw,
Casting him a lone outlaw.

With rapid beats, he wings his way
To the edges of the day,
To village ditch and salty bay:
Like a hobo had to stray,
And dibble, dabble, with his spear
Till his habitat is clear.
He probes and prods for winter fare,
Danger ever chasing near.

When spring returns the blithe outcast;
Pear-shaped eggs are laid at last,
Clear pools reflect the heaven vast,
Where he flies; the snipe, so fast.
From sunrise into ebbing light,
He duth shower pure delight;
Out drumming his romantic flight,
Far beyond the winter night.

# THE SHEPHERD'S HUT

The shepherd's hut redundant now;
On iron wheels, in disrepair:
These modern times no longer need
Twentyfour-seven lambing care.

Towed to its final resting place,
A country park where harebells sway,
To be restored by kindred folk,
Where swallows fly and children play.

The old bed where the shepherd slept
Near faithful dog, a friend sublime.
A stove to warm an orphan's milk,
When lambs were born at lambing time.

Cold, starry nights and silver moon,
The bleating flock, the foxes' bark,
The shepherd and his collie bold,
Rise to the singing of the lark.

Refurbished now, the shepherd's hut, -
A relic of our heritage.
A plaque tells of its history,
The story of a bygone age.

# TANGLED WOODLAND

Tangled woodland, still and waiting
For the sap of life to rise,
Boughs asunder, still reflecting
Winter in the dreary skies.

Tangled woodland pointing skywards,
New growth ready to burst through.
When the temperature is warmer
Nature will come through anew.

Suddenly, a morning's sunrise
Shine upon a whole new scene;
Woodland blooms in rainbow colours
Brighten up the shades of green.

All creatures of the woodland,
Wide eyed, now, and multiply.
High above the sap has risen
To the blueness of the sky.

# AN EAGLE'S TALE

We waited there excitedly,
We scoured the sullen sky,
We knew about the eagle's nest
And where the eagles fly.

We wondered, would we see the birds -
Would one come into view
Then suddenly high in the clouds
We saw the form we knew.

The male sea-eagle circled high
As high as any lark;
His white tail glistened in the murk -
His 'barn door' wings so dark.

And as we watched, he hurtled down,
Wings closing as he went;
He landed on the eyrie tree
And there seemed quite content.

The exchange came so quick and sure
It almost beat the eye.
The female left the eyrie tree
And faded in the sky.

Across the hills she disappeared
To search a nearby loch.
She left her suitor there to brood
The future eagle stock.

The eagles fly o'er Mull once more
And all the Hebrides,
And could there be a finer sight,
A finer sight than these?

# WINTER CAST

The woodland now is green again,
The pretty flowers peep through.
The sky above is blue again
And everything seems new.

The little bees are in the air;
The cuckoo's on his way,
And cricket will be played again
On ev'ry Saturday.

The thrush is sitting in the hedge
On eggs of speckled blue.
And in the pond the waterhen
Builds her old nest anew.

The sun is bursting through once more;
And gnats dance in its rays.
The daylight hours are stretching out,
Towards the summer days.

The thought of winter fading fast;
A blessed year in store.
The winter cloak is cast at last,
Lambs gambol as of yore.

# NOT ONE SWALLOW

Although the day was fine and fair,
With blue skies overhead,
Not one swallow was seen or heard,
No tears of joy were shed.

Just one swallow, just one swallow;
We searched above the lea,
But none were seen and I did think
That all had died at sea.

The clouds rolled over tender skies
And shadows fell to earth,
The ash trees waited cuckoo cries
And waited cuckoo birth.

These shadows that on river fell
Were shed by honest trees,
And there did spring a breeze to whip
The wind into a breeze.

Where nettles rose at summer's edge
And harvest fair flew high,
I did remember lemon days
And swallows in the sky.

# TOAD

From torpid sleep down winter's well,
The toad emerged into the night;
And with her sight, her taste, her smell
Immersed herself in bright moonlight.

Into the damp, cold, starry, glare,
With jerky steps she ventured out,
And with her wit began to steer
Beyond the drain's old water spout.

Towards the magic of her pond,
An epic journey for a toad;
Where kingcups raise their head beyond
The siren voices of the road.

## ARISE THE SPRING

When spring bursts through, all heaven stirs and sings
With open heart, the vagaries of things.
Of soil and bud and storm; and blossoms o'er
The old pear-tree, so gnarled this many year.
Now that spring is here the sap will bubble,
Thunder blacks the sky and there is trouble:
Bouncing hail that doomed pink, pear-tree petals
Flattens the bright daffodils and nettles.
Spring's sap will rise and skies will turn to blue,
The cuckoo will return with much ado.
Frogs make their bid and snails enjoy the rain,
Song-thrush and blackbird chant their own refrain.
Springtime has come with butterfly and bee:
The sun bursts through to praise spring's dignity.

# THE NIGHTINGALE

Suddenly he was there.
Dropped in from the stars:
Just a croak at first
To cloak what he is really about.
A croak to let us know of his
Annoyance at our audacity
To enter his domain.
The domain of the gods.

We strain our eyes,
He can see us.
We know of each others presence,
But we can't see him. Not yet.
When he decides he will show
Himself, but for now
He lets his song work
The magic for us.

Just a chance would do!
Now he's further along the track,
Amid the wild roses
And cobwebbed nettles.
Amid the misty evening.
He is singing again.
Now's our chance.

# UNDER THE WOOD

Before I came into
This world of mirth and woe,
Song thrushes sang
And they still do.

The stars shone in the skies
Above my ancestors.
They spent their lives
And shed their tears.

This ancient English wood
Has secrets yet untold -
The heathen's god
Grew sick and cold.

Great oaks have spread and died
And deer have fallen still.
Those hunters cried
As was their will.

Now winds this windless track
With no more energy,
Echoes bounce back
In sympathy.

A tiny piece of pot
More dignified than man,
Pokes through this plot,
Beneath this span.

# THE NIGHTJAR

Thunder crashed upon the earth
And struck the heavens black;
Bells rang out from heaven's tower,
Sent the storm to blast each flower
And ev'ry forest track.
Fierce lightning flashed across the heath,
Smote everything we saw,
Amid the gale a Nightjar sang,
From heathered home its churring rang
And we were filled with awe.

The wind howled, the heavens spat
With brimstone and with fire;
Yet through it all this song we heard,
This haunting song of this shy bird
Reeled on and did not tire.
This song we loved and marvelled at,
Yet we were wet and worn;
There seemed to be a harmony
As nature played her symphony;
Out there our love was born.

All the forest shook with fear,
Fell dark as ebony;
About our heads, just where we stood,
The storm played havoc in the wood
And boasted victory.
But there amid the evening drear
This mighty bird did sing,
It sang in triumph over all,
Until alone the bird did call;
It was the sweetest thing.

# THE BLACK BUSH

The track of flowers and bramble briars;
With many birds perched on phone wires;
Where darkness flows in, thick and fast,
The clouds push out the sun at last.

The day is tired, in need of sleep,
And nature bids its secrets keep,
Within the silence of the brush,
Sweet music bursts out from a bush.

The black bush throws a golden sound;
The nightingale finale bound
It's song of rivers, dreams and love;
Much brighter than the moon above.

# A BIRD IN MICKLE WOOD

Where have you been all winter through?
No sign or any sound from you.
All winter through the woods were bare,
All winter through you were not there.

That haunting song for poets gone,
Those unique notes were yours alone;
And you had flown to southern climes,
Here you were missed a thousand times.

Then, when new sap rose in the bud
Green leaves appeared in Mickle wood.
Amid the sunshine and the rain
We heard your murmurings again.

We found you there where few souls do
Out on a limb and in full view,
Rampant was your glorious song;
May it resound all summer long.

And echo through the winter too
When ev'ry tree is bare bar yew.
May your enchanting notes live on
Lest we forget your wondrous song.

# IN THE SPRING OF THE YEAR

I will see you again.
In the spring of the year,
When robins are nesting
In the bole of the pear.
I will hold you once more
When the primroses bloom,
In the spring of the year
When the swallows fly home.

*When my darling comes home,*
*When my darling comes home.*
*In the spring of the year*
*When my darling comes home.*

We will walk the worn tracks
All around the old farm
When the swallows return
To their nests in the barn.
In the spring of the year
When the violets bloom
I will skip like a lamb
When my darling comes home.

# THE INVISIBLE DOG

Of silent whim, unseen with naked eye,
Wool and hide are ruptured to the spleen.
Soft eyes, entombed, will never see the sky:
Ovine, hircine, bovine and porcine.
A plague without a soul or sense of shame,
To curse the lips of all who know its name.

Men and machine, in tandem, rape the view:
Beauties to burn, limbs all akimbo.
Diktat fries uneatable barbeque -
Dante's inferno, Britannia afire -
Their place of rest, the red-hot cinder pyre.

'What happened to the lambs?' A stranger says;
'The cows and pigs, sheep and nanny goats?'
'All gone!' I say. Alas, these many days!'
Icons of state, broken at their roots.
A desert land all void of farmyard stock;
The invisible dog has run amok.

# WHERE THE BITTERN HANGS HIS HAT

We heard the boom of a bittern
As we strolled along the track;
We heard the boom of a bittern
As we made our journey back.

The sound of spring was on the wing
As the old bird boomed all day,
It filled our ears, this mystic thing
With a springtime roundelay.

Amid the reeds he hangs his hat
When the kettle's on the boil.
He pokes his head into the sky -
Blows his trumpet with a smile.

Somehow he gathers up his puff
To summon his haunting cry
And skulks around his marshy lair
With a twinkle in his eye.

We logged the grunt of the bittern,
A sound that is rarely heard;
The boom and grunt of a bittern
From a bird that is absurd.

# THE OAK-WOOD

Across the ploughed and barren field
Where shadows drift and skylarks sing:
Lies on the skyline, an oak-wood,
Which is a many splendored thing.

Tall trunks in dark formation stand,
And contrast greatly with the sky:
And contrast stately with the land;
They stand and watch the world go by.

And when the sun shines overhead,
The trees themselves seem nearer too;
When nature lifts them from the dead,
They dress up in a finer hue.

# OAKS OF ENGLAND

These English oaks that stand sublime,
Have seen a man grow in their time,
Have seen two hundred years go by
And tasted immortality.

Both silently and with great noise;
Like giants true have touched the skies,
And they have seen a landscape plea
For no more human slavery.

In virgin soil a plow shear bit
And lapwings eggs rolled into it,
Now great machines like armies ply
Their worth with little dignity.

In oak-tree shade a nation stands
With jaded bones and guilty hands;
And turmoil in society
Boils over with hostility.

How long, I say, O mighty trees
Have you to trudge these English leas?
All seasons fall like vanity,
O steer us free from anarchy.

As for today, the new lambs dwell
Where once the Kings of England fell;
O trees of oak long may you reign
And make this England great again.

## SPRING

Oh spring, such majesty you bring our way,
And stir once more, each nook, each brook, each tree.
You raise a Lazarus to life each day,
And fill the lanes and meadows with beauty.
Each bee, each butterfly out on the hill
Shows off a splendour to the world around,
And greener now, each forest, hedge and rill,
Joy rings the same from skylark, sky and ground.
So, in this clime of solitude and grace,
Where blossoms drink the dew each new day brings
And swallows wing again to their birthplace,
I hope this spring will bring the best of springs.
A splendid spring, like heaven would relieve
This earth bound falsity of make believe.

## ORD GROVE

The calmest of the calmest days
That ever spring did bring,
Brought me, my love, to Ord's green grove,
Where robins sweetly sing.

Its fertile floor was covered o'er
With blooms of varied hues;
White anemones caught my gaze
With softest bluebell, blues.

Shy violets and primroses
Shone from the dank, damp soil;
I sank beneath a lofty oak
And rested for awhile.

The sky began to spit, my love,
Above a tractor's drone,
I looked around to ev'ry sound
And did not feel alone.

As everywhere was spring's idea
Of pleasure to my eye;
A willow-warbler softly sang
Beneath a daunting sky.

As I engaged that youthful scene,
Many a thing I found,
Shelled hazel-nuts and blackbird's eggs
Were scattered on the ground.

Beside a raided rabbit's hole
Three baby ones lay cold,
They died there in a blinded state,
All, but a few days old.

Ahead of me sly jays called out
And bade me go away,
But I walked on and on, my love,
Exploring that spring day.

# GREY BLOCKS

Grey blocks,
Sinister in the sky,
Where clouds just pass by.

Acres of glass similar to sheep
Are piled one on one
And so on,
Giving a ghostly appearance
To the whole ugly view.

Stark are its edges,
Beyond these is space,
Within these is an existence
For an unfortunate race.

Inside are housed moving death traps,
They shudder up and down;
To the whims of the inmates,
To the whims of a clown.
Piercing through human experience,
But not considering them.

Lonely people with lonely ideas
Pass their time away from bird song
And refreshing rain.

They never set eyes on a brimstone butterfly
Drinking its fill from a swaying clover flower,
They hear not the gentle ripple of a mountain
Stream as it passes through valleys
Of limitless peace.

They do see grey blocks,
Sinister in the sky,
Where clouds just pass by.

And hear water dying in the pipes
As if in pain.

Who are they really,
Anonymous, faceless, reading, nagging,
Nowhere to pray,
There must always be somewhere to pray.

Areas like cardboard boxes,
Units like blocks:
So far from the meadow bathed in dew;
So far from the hawthorn and the yew.

They must be made of flesh and blood,
And have identities:
It is hard to say;
Time goes by there at the same pace as elsewhere,
So they become cold and old.

What will their memorial be,
Grey blocks,
Sinister in the sky,
Where clouds just pass by?

# THE WHITE SHEET

The dead elms stand like martyrs,
Like tombstones dark and drear:
Like loved ones deep in mourning,
With shocks of greying hair.

The sun dies with a whimper,
Well beaten by the night;
And out across the hillside,
A farmstead sheds a light.

The daylight's dying embers
Are less now than a spark;
A greyer tone the white takes on,
For cometh now the dark.

The oaks meet with the skyline
And heavy seems their sighs,
The ditches and the ridges,
Now blend in with the skies.

The cornfields are so peaceful,
Beneath the winter sheet,
And grow in strength for harvest;
The barley and the wheat.

This earth has much to offer
The rich man and the poor,
For soon will rise the morning
And soon will wake the thaw.

# FALSE LOVE

False love you wither me,
You steal my breath away;
For heaven's sake deliver me
From this untimely clay.

Just like November's sun,
You're false as any dream;
You flaunt a spring that will not come,
You hide behind a gleam.

Why does the blackbird sing?
No spring is on the wing;
False love 'tis winter that you bring
And with it winter's sting.

Why do you deceive me
And make me feel secure?
When there is no security,
Of this I can be sure.

The song thrush sings alone,
Maybe he's happy now;
He will be bitten to the bone
When winter brings the snow.

False love who do you fool?
False spring where will you hide?
No doubt you'll find some draughty hole
To sell your bitter pride.

# DEAD ELMS

They died like a sunset
In the midst of their glory;
They died like a mem'ry
Of days long since gone.
They died like a melody
That rang though the forest,
They died like the waves
That fall on the sand.

Parched now and bleached now,
Like cast away sinners;
Rigid they stand
So bleak on the sky.
The leaves that they bear
Were shed by another
And lodged by the wind
From a faraway world.

Once they were green
And rose to their harvest;
Once they were living
But now they are dead.
Dead in the sunlight.
Blind, tatty objects,
Weird statues they look
Of a faraway age.

Their shadows fall lifeless
Over the city,
Their shadows fall limbless
Over the vale.
They do not sway
With the beauty they used to,
And pilgrims walk on
Beneath their dry boughs.

# HARE ON THE HIGHROAD

The car, the speed, the night was dark,
The hare was running free.
The speed, the car was on his back
He sobbed, 'Don't murder me'.

A thump that drives a man insane,
A shriek to make him cry;
And there a rushing through the night,
A hare about to die.

And now he comes to haunt me so,
A nightmare in the night;
And in his eyes are cries of pain
And never more delight.

# YONDER COMET

Yonder, a comet! Burning bright,
In the cold vastness of the night;
Beyond the realms of man's intrigue,
You blaze your trail from league to league.
You are a Jupiter, a Mars!
And shine more brightly than the stars,
Insatiable is what you are,
More hungry than a hungry star.
When man first rose his ugly head,
He thought of you as something dread;
A brute in heaven's fine array,
A fickle thief who'd lost his way:
And when man spluttered with his pen,
He saw you as a demon then,
A raiding knight to rape the sky,
A flying, screaming, horse of Troy.
Now man has grown so clever too
He nearly knows the half of you,
Amid your searing, gleaming glow
Is but a dirty ball of snow.

# THE SKYLARK

Sing out your praises far up into heaven,
Your body flung high like a stone from a sling;
Into the morning the songs of the shepherds
Will roll from your tongue as you quiver and sing.

Your music will stir the angels of glory,
They will render to God your sweet melody;
Wild  minstrel so mighty, wizard of fortune,
O, what is it like to be happy and free?

And how does it feel to have conquered the earth,
To fall like a bolt, like a star from the sky?
You, who can talk with the angels of glory,
And walk with us mortals and lie where we lie.

# THE BLACK BIRD

Singing from the highest spire
Was a bird in black attire,
When the sun shone on his bill,
He sang sweetly there until
Darkness fell upon the day;
Night then whisked him far away
To his tree, there to retire,
Splendidly in black attire.

# RIVER WATCH

The willows are hollow,
Reeds murmur and moan,
The sedges soon follow;
The winds not alone.

The rain is just ripping
The mist from the sun,
The river's forbidding
The evening to come.

The heavy clouds cover
The moon's gentle light,
The night birds discover
The depth of the night.

The water is sparkling,
The shadows obey;
The moments are hailing
The glint of the day.

Awakes a new dawning;
The night drains with fear,
And bright is the morning
With song in the air.

# THE BLACK SENTINEL

Wizard of velvet in feather and voice,
Bird of my passion and bird of my choice;
You are a prophet and so can foretell
The longings of nature, black sentinel.
You sing, sweetly sing, your golden refrain,
And sanctify souls in sunshine and rain:
Your home's a meadow, your castle a tree,
I envy you blackbird! What you of me?
Nobly you strive with your dusky brown maid,
Tending your charges in apple green shade;
You whisper wisdom till light leaves the sky,
And teach them music and how they should fly.
O let me dwell in your magical dell
And there find contentment, black sentinel.

# PAINTED LADIES FROM AFRICA

Painted ladies from Africa;
Gaudy colours aglow;
They remonstrate from gate to gate
And skirt each bright hedgerow.

They flit and fly 'twixt earth and sky,
The swiftest of their breed
And love displays mid bridleways
Are made at awesome speed.

They flutter by, each butterfly
On nimble, rainbow wing,
Nectar feeding where I'm weeding;
They tap the sap of spring.

# O LOVELY DAY

O lovely day spread forth your wings,
Embrace my love and lovely things,
And on the moonbeams of your night
Let me espy her shining bright.

O lovely day on silver hill,
There she be seated, silent, still:
Green are her valleys, wide and green
And blue her waters in between.

The many sequins of her dress
At each day's dawn are always fresh,
At each day's night are moulded true,
And at each season, bright and new.

Roll back the curtains with the tide,
There in the sand the creatures hide;
Push back the clouds that float on high
And count the stars that roam the sky.

When winter sags with mystery;
O lovely day I'll yearn for thee;
So then will I set forth a dove
To search the valleys for my love.

# NIGHTINGALE MOON

O the moon is full tonight,
Full of light and symmetry,
Thus she shines her magic light
Over hill and summer tree.
Mellow glints in woodland glade,
Wakes the heart of nightingale,
Soon he stirs to serenade
Mistress moon above the vale.

My fair maid, he seems to sing,
Rise and fall in sympathy,
Catch me as I dip my wing
Silhouetted in my tree.
Softest rays caress his brow
Permeating from above,
Nightingale sings from his bough
His enchanting song of love.

All the creatures of the night
Scurry with their eyes aglow;
Mistress moon's seductive light
Brings bird to his crescendo.
Daylight rises from its sleep,
Now all the world is woken.
Bird and moon their secrets keep;
At last the spell is broken.

# KING HARRY

King Harry, King Harry,
Up in the pear tree,
You sing a sweet ditty,
So pretty, it be.

Amid its white petals
Rests your tiny nest,
With grey pates emerging
At nature's behest!

The sun beats your feathers,
Brilliance astound,
Red, white, black and yellow
Rich colours abound.

King Harry, King Harry
Amid thistle down,
You tarry and swagger
To show off your crown!

# SHE'S A FOOL

She's a fool and she shows it,
She's a fool and she knows it;
She flashes her deep brown eyes.
Ev'ry time that I see her
She makes me feel a winner
With her head held to the skies.

She's a creature of habit,
And can run like a rabbit;
Wears her black coat all the year!
And when I go to see her
She takes me out to dinner,
And seems not to have a care.

She's full of pranks and prances,
And sometimes even dances.
No, she doesn't cramp my style!
She bathes in lush, green grasses,
And nods to those who passes;
She's a winner by a mile.

She has a lot to offer,
And ignores those who scoff her:
She's a lady and of course,
Me thinks she's not a phoney
Nor just a silly pony;
Nay, she's one hunk of a horse.

# SUMMER DREAM

I feast mine eyes on nature's things,
And in the air a thousand wings
Beat out a thousand tunes.
The nooks around this noble place
Are filled with magic and with grace,
And nature's bold fortunes.

The shafts of night stretch into light
And what was black is now pure white
And wakes a summer dream.
And out there where the winter shed
Its shabby coat of russet-red,
There tumbles one sunbeam.

The mist will bide its time today
And hide amidst the clouds that play
Above the racing brook.
All weather-beaten on the hill
The oak grove stands so bold and still
And hikers pause to look.

The silent grass and butterflies
Look upwards to the distant skies
With vision ever sure;
Pink roses glow, row after row,
And singing fills the air just now
With water running pure.

And when the morning sun breaks through
The whole of nature shines anew
At heaven's gentle pull.
And when the great trees shake before
The gushing sap and floral floor,
'Tis summer beautiful.

# SPIDER IN YOUR SHED

Behind your back a spider lurks,
A spider dark and dread,
Behind your back it bides its time
Somewhere in your old shed.

The goat was torn to bits last night
And sets of eight were found;
It was the spider from your shed
Out on its beastly round.

Behind the disused tins of paint,
Behind the old armchair,
Is where the spider lurks and waits,
Is where it has its lair.

The monster's legs are hairy black,
Its eyes are red and raw;
Its poison fangs are like steel tongs
And sharper than a claw.

Behind your back a spider lurks;
The old black cat is dead.
There is a groan, a fearsome moan
Coming from your old shed!

# BRECKLAND BIRD

Waiting for the dusk to fall
As the sun sinks in the sky;
Waiting for the bird to call,
Waiting for the bird to fly.

Late July down summer's lane,
Shadows dicing with the sun;
Nature's first flush on the wane,
Growing season nearly done.

Breckland and the dark, green fir,
Darker still this windless eve;
Moths fly on the balmy air,
Swallows through the dimness weave.

Then the bird begins to call
As the moon begins to shine,
Its jarring notes rise and fall
Over bush and stately pine.

Silently it twists and glides
Like a large, black butterfly:
In this realm where it abides:
Bereft of the city's cry.

# POTATO HARVESTER

It rumbled on through years of toil
Lifting spuds from the Hepworth soil,
Then it was dumped and left to rot,
In quite a lovely beauty spot.

It lingered there as time went by,
And rotted there beneath the sky;
Pied wagtails found it had appeal,
They built their nest above a wheel.

The years went by and then one day
The heap of junk was towed away
To make its final journey home,
Fit for scrap and ultimate doom.

The eye-sore of the bridle track
Has left and brought the beauty back.
The lane shows off a greener hue
With no blue, rotting hulk in view.

Horse riders are no longer shy
To pass the spot where it did lie,
And wagtails without more ado
Have flown away to pastures new.

# ISLANDS OF JOY

Red stags so beautiful, sniff at the air,
The sweet Jura air that none can compare.
Eagles above are upwind and soaring,
Choughs on the crags sound like the wind calling.
The breakers crash down so wild on the rocks,
And curlews wisp in with sanderling flocks.
The Strand stretches out far into the sea;
Island of Ilay, I hear you call me.
Hen Harriers search the marshes of Oa,
O to be with them my heart longs to go.
Island of Jura, sweet haven of joy,
My thoughts drift with your Hebridean sky.
The ferry awaits at Tarbert for me,
I shall return like the swallow to thee.

# SUNSET CITY

I see a city in the sky
Where mountains watch the day go by.
I see a fountain in a square
And happy people strolling there.

I see a city and its hills
And blooms amid the window sills,
Winding roads like blood-red ribbons
Punctuate the golden heavens.

Amid the smiling faces there
Are the different races there,
All living in sweet harmony
In their fair city of the sky.

This city seems to fade away
Just at the closing of each day.
The city falls as falls the night
It tumbles down, sinks out of sight.

So where do all the buildings go,
The city square, the avenue?
The streets of red and burnished gold,
Just vanish, disappear, unfold.

Yet when the sunrise comes again,
The city wakes and lives again;
For a short time, a little while,
Until the sun gives up its smile.

# CHANGING SCENE

I can hear the great oaks rustling
In the July ev'ning breeze,
I can see the wheat fields moving
Like the waves of distant seas.

I can sense the harvest coming:
Ripe acorns and golden corn;
I can see the swallows skimming,
Catching flies above it all.

I can hear the combines droning,
Gathering the ripened ears.
I can hear the workers joking
In a harvest which is theirs.

Soon the picture will be altered
With the bounty safely in:
Then the summer will be over
And the winter night begin.

Then the plough will tear the stubble
And the gulls will search the soil;
Soon the new seed will be scattered
Which will lie and rest awhile.

Then the scene will be much bleaker,
No cotton clouds flying high;
Trees all leafless in the winter
And no swallows in the sky.

# THE HARVEST- MOON

The harvest-moon is round and bright
And shuns the darkness of the night,
And all the world that lies beneath
Is bathed within her silver wreath.

And all the world that needs to know
Has an empathy with her glow.
The tides that flit around the shore
Are governed by celestial law.

The deer that stalk the nearby hill,
The church itself, its pinnacle;
And all the fowl that fly by night
Are silhouetted in her light.

Lovers stroll with intimate air
Along the lanes the moon lays bare,
And harvest time is at its height,
High summer, when the moon is bright.

## LINES

I see them now, the wasps, on fallen fruit;
Jaws moving as they chew their fleshy food,
And walking as they do in jerky steps.
Backwards and forwards, to left and to right,
Eyes so cruel, their faces black and mean.
Their antenna probe and pry before them,
And when they leave, they fly, and fly with rage
To torture and to menace what they can.
Bluebottles and green-bottles settle there,
To take their share mid a poisonous foe,
And from the sun the butterflies float down
To sip what'er decays upon the ground,
And in the air I hear the insect hum,
And I can smell the summer crying out.

# WHERE BUZZARDS FLY

What time has past
Since this track was flat?
What forces did concur
To mould these awesome hills?
Was love there then
Or redress, or ravaging peace
And eternal change?

Was man a mere glint in
Nature's eye?

Yet we are here, and now
Can see the beauty.
We hear the roaring Dee,
Where rainbows appear and
Re-appear in their glory.
We roam the slate-tipped
Towns, sleep and eat there.

You stride off, little steps;
Off with a purpose. An
Aqueduct, a canal, chiselled
Out of the rock. Amid great
Forces of old. Forces that
Now sleep where buzzards fly.

# SEPTEMBER

Land of berries, corn and vine
This is your stage;
Rebuild the sagging earth
In this your age,
So birth can find rebirth
And turn the page.

There are now more shades of red
Than shades of green;
Docks match the copper-beech
And blood the scene.
September swallows teach
Their young to preen.

Thistle down, like summer snow
Floats in the air,
And on a dying day
Of falling cheer,
A cricket chirps away
Upon a tare.

A lone whitethroat flits about
An elder bush.
It feeds where once it sang
With mellow thrush
Now bright, black jewels hang
Amid the hush.

Chestnuts lie deep in the womb
Of mother tree;
And wait the midwife frost
To bear them free.
Soon summer will be lost
With leaf and bee.

Grasses at park's edge have known
A brighter sun;
And cornfields are now black
The harvest done
Yet nature has the knack
To overcome.

Doves salute the autumn air
And butterflies
Drink down their last farewell
As summer dies.
And swifts no longer dwell
In changing skies.

Store of bounty, flour and wine,
Blow loud your horn,
Rejuvenate again
The golden corn,
Replace a summer slain
With life reborn.

# THE GEESE OF ANNANDALE

The geese are in the meadow
Eating grass so green.
The geese are in the meadow,
An idyllic scene.

The geese are on the water
All paddling away,
The geese are on the water,
An idyllic day.

The geese are on the island
Honking as they do.
The geese are on the island
An idyllic view.

# AUTUMN AND BEYOND

The beanfield has grown fat with care
As autumn seizes one more year
To turn the page through seed and grain
To set to life this land again.
As autumn shadows fall to earth
Wild swans fly in with all their worth
From frozen spheres and Arctic night,
As robins, red, sing with delight.
For now the blue skies reign above
This good, old country that I love.

The latent sun is still aglow,
I feel it through my window now.
This window where I sit and stare
At nature's wonderland out there;
I dream of snow and outer space
Where fieldfares wing from their birthplace,
To echo over these green lands
When winter bites, where autumn stands.
With beanfield gone and swallows flown,
Dame Nature wears a scanty gown.

# TITCHWELL TWITCHERS

Titchwell bookshop, twitchers look
At the birdies in a book -
Amble down to marshy hide
Where the specimens abide.
Through their lenses peep and peer,
Birdie common, birdie rare!
Spoonbills, ruff and avocets
Make a day with no regrets.

Starlings voyage across the sky,
Swarm like bees and multiply.
Storm erupts at eventide,
Rainbow ladder is the guide
Up to heavens burnished gold
Where the sacred lakes unfold,
And where twitchers, on demise,
Tick off birds of paradise.

# A FLAMINGO

Wet, uncaring semi-sky,
Raw and dank the dykes below;
Bleak lagoon in fickle light,
Rippling waters ebb and flow.

There amid the fleeting winds
Seeding reed-beds dance and sway
To a sad and mournful song -
Eerie voices in the bay.

All within and all about
Whirling waders rise and fall,
Wildfowl and bold birds of prey
Search for food where curlews call.

Homeward we, at end of day,
Clouds all dull and indigo;
Out there in the murky clay,
A lone bright, pink flamingo.

# WATERCOURSE

The stream runs free when life is young
And spring rides on the vine,
The water gurgles on its way
And all the world is fine.
The sky is blue, all nature new;
No clogging of the soul,
The birds sing free in ev'ry tree
And all the world seems whole.

Alas the weeds begin to form
As summer has her day;
The water flows not quite so sure
And falters on its way.
The clouds seem heavy overhead
As life ebbs with the stream,
And many butterflies are dead
Or lost with summer's dream.

At last the fall hits watercourse,
Decay hangs on the vine,
And in the shadows deep remorse
Seeks out this soul of mine.
The church bell tolls a last farewell
To nature's golden rays,
And old men dream their futile dreams
Amid the cold, wet clays.

# LAPWINGS IN A BEAN FIELD

Coming down, one after one
In the fading light of evening;
After searching for worms
And insects all day long.

Now they descend,
One after one, to the bean field
For a well earned rest.
Cold winds blowing,
Broad wings descending.

They call "Pee-wit", one after one;
Like workers returning home,
Sons of the soil.
Lapwings, black and white,
Ripples of light.
In the fading of the day.

In they come, down they come,
One after one,
Quickly they run,
Crests extended,
Through the dark green beans,
As if a magic flute has sounded,
Calling them to rest,
Independently they come,
Together they arrive to sleep
And fox watch.

## ROBINS

I never found their nest, the robins
Although I saw them come and go all spring through,
Bits of moss, later bits of worm,
They all left, went away, save one, a cock bird.
He stayed, bobbing about near the little white gate,
All dressed in brown he was.
Then as the summer drove on he changed,
He became a new bird, red of breast - a robin.
And in September he sang to me,
We had become friends.
His little bright eye would glance my way.
He sang sweetly from the buddleia tree through
The coming of the butterflies and the harvest.
He kept on singing sweetly from sunrise or
Before 'til sunset and beyond, bright as a new idea.

# APPLE

Did it draw breath when on the tree?
Is it downcast now it is free?
Lying helpless, sore, forsaken,
Face of fire yet to awaken.

A dying life, a living soul,
Not just an apple in a bowl.
Its body shrivels up and dies,
Its inner self beats on and lives.

Does it remember days of growth
In the fair orchard of its youth?
And is it sad or mystified
In losing all its former pride?

Does it recall the insect hum?
The dew, the dusk, the morning sun?
Does it now dream a summer dream
Of pleasant rains and dawns between?

There deep within its very core
The pips await an open door,
When each will claim its liberty
And climb into an apple-tree.

# TREES

The trees of the forest
Are black and unyielding.
They sleep forever or
They never sleep.

They recreate themselves
And wander at their will.
They use the cattle of the
Forest to disperse their seed.
It's a ploy!

They are our masters.
They were here before us
And will be here long after
We have been forgotten
By the birds.

We must have them to breathe,
At all costs.

# OCTOBER ROBIN

Arcade of light, this realm of joy,
A still day bright and free;
The blueness of the bluest sky,
The greenness of each tree.
I sing beneath this handsome oak
Whose limbs stretch far and wide;
But soon its winter coat will soak
And I, where will I hide?

If only now could last a while,
The wind remain a breeze;
This perfect day which brings a smile
Could be more than a tease.
I sing now to the morning sun,
I welcome its warm breath,
And know quite soon north winds will come
And bring the winter death.

For now I will soak up this joy,
And count each fluffy cloud;
And watch the last lone butterfly
Before the winter shroud.
I sing my soft, sweet winter song
When all around decays;
I sing my song all winter long
And dream of summer days.

# THE SPIRIT

Where light as bright as any light
That ever found a day,
Where crystal clear, the noble air
Rejoices in the bay:
Where gulls that called and seas that mauled
The distant dance of men;
Is where I saw her crystal clear,
A shining diadem.

Where moonlit rocks and far flung flocks
Of birds upon a stream,
Where hill hid tides bring down the skies
And ev'ry one moonbeam:
Where mountains rank high on the bank
Of earth's amazing scene,
Is where she spreads her wings and flies
Just like a fairy queen.

Where forests bright, stretch into night,
Where oaks grow old and wise,
Where wild deer roam and branches groan,
Where cry the woodland cries;
Where summer sold, turns into gold,
Where treasures lay in store,
Is where she roams all on her own,
Is where she reigns for sure.

## FRIEND DEPARTED

I heard his fluent song at first
Then twigged his sparking eye.
His breast was turning brown to red
As summertime sped by.

And we were pals, the two of us;
He fed out of my palm,
And followed me where'er I went
"Fraid I should come to harm.

And we had an understanding:
I spoke, he turned his head,
And he listened so intently
To everything I said.

One morning when I chanced outdoors
No robin could be found,
Just a pile of blood-stained feathers
Were clinging to the ground.

I shall miss my little robin,
And miss his cheerful song.
As summer turns to autumn now,
The dark days will seem long.

# KNOCKING THE BAT DOWN

The night was filled with bat-like clouds,
All winging through the sky;
And on the trees hung bat-like shapes
As I drove slowly by.

The night was blacker than the dark,
Much blacker than the sky,
And leaves all wilted and forlorn
Went on wearily by.

A dog howled like a frightened child,
And chilled my very spine;
As I approached along the lane
The beast again did whine.

Then suddenly from out the blue,
As I edged to the scene,
The torso of a bat emerged
And crashed against the screen.

I stopped abruptly and walked back;
There laid the little mite,
It looked just like a dead mushroom
All shrivelled in the night.

I wondered how this could have been,
This miracle of flight;
With all its radar functioning,
Had fallen from the night.

This tiny, furry pipistrelle
A mere two inches long,
Was dying in the roadway now
For nothing it did wrong.

I picked it up, this tiny thing,
Its heart was beating fast;
And still and limp it rested there
All safe within my grasp.

I placed it down beside of me,
It woke up from its tomb;
Its pin like eyes were brighter now
Just as I reached my home.

I gently held it in my hands,
And stroked its tiny head;
It did not try to fly away
But shew its teeth instead.

And it looked just like an old man,
With methylated eyes,
Like a ferret or a weasel,
A witch wrought with demise.

It reminded me of chicken legs
Or a festering bumblebee;
It reminded me of witchcraft
For nought else could I see.

I carried it with loving care
And placed it in my shed;
When daylight broke its darkened veil
The little bat was dead.

I placed the tiny, lifeless thing
Out on a low brick wall,
And later on the self-same day
My daughter paid a call.

Her face was taunt, her eyes were sad
And moist with many a tear;
She asked me how the bat had died
And how come it was there.

I told her of the tragic tale
And of the creature's fate;
It's flimsy wings looked just like lace
Held to the world out straight,

She fixed her gaze upon the sky
And I could plainly see,
That in her mind there flew the bat,
Contented, happy, free.

# RUTLAND WATER

Those little boats that sparkle
Above the rainbow-trout,
Are cradled in a valley
Where birds wheel all about.

The lapwings and the seagulls
All shimmer in the sun;
As sheep pass their days away
And hosts of fishes run.

This green and pleasant picture,
Where man dreams all the day;
Is Rutland's lake of pleasure,
Is where the fishes play.

Wings beat a million feathers
Sun beats a thousand fins,
The fishermen do linger
As on a spider spins.

They sit and wait, pulse racing;
The water deep and wide,
The hours tick by like moments,
Somewhere the fishes hide.

# THE STORM

Clouds bolt across the sky
Like horses mad with fear:
Fingers of the wind strike out
To pillage, cut and tear.

Trees are blown asunder
Like cities of the past
The howling of the thunder
Seems like a woman cast.

Shattered shacks shoot skyward
Just like forgotten dreams,
All searching for a heaven
However hard it seems.

Horses cling together
All stricken by the storm,
Out in the stormy weather
A million miles from home.

Heaven points a finger
With brimstone and with fire;
With torment, helter-skelter,
With all of heaven's power.

## OLD NESTS

Now the trees are without leaf
And the hedges stark and bare:
One can see the old bird nests
All torn, forsaken there.

One a thrush and one a wren,
Near the ground a blackcap's too;
All were shaded, sheltered, safe
Until the north winds blew.

Now they are caught unawares
In the bare bones of the hedge.
Were they found by boys or jays
Or did the young birds fledge?

Soon new leaves will reappear;
Nests all new will hide from view,
One a thrush and one a wren
And one a blackcap's too.

# TITMICE

You build your home in briar or broom
And line it well with feathers;
You lay your eggs, one ev'ry day,
And hope to stay all weathers.

Your baby chicks may number ten,
And all of you are snug there;
And when they fly, you fly with them
At the back end of the year.

You trip like monkeys through the trees
When distant be your labours,
To forage in the chilling breeze
And sleep with all your neighbours.

# ROE DEER

As I stopped by, that dark night,
Three roe in a gateway stood;
They seemed bemused by my light
So far from their darkened wood.

They stood ungainly and peered
Like kids or lambs fill'd with glee;
And then by magic appeared
Another to join the said three.

I watched, as if in a dream;
Their ears and tails twitch away.
And then a sudden moonbeam
Reminded them of the day.

They skipped along and bounded
Beyond the beam of my light,
As if some horn had sounded
Out from the depths of the night.

# THE SNOWMAN

Who would dare to build a snowman?
Image of God, image of man!
No life to live, no death to die,
Water to earth, vapour to sky.

No soul, no immortality
And yet it seems to stare at me.
Who dares to build a snowman here?
Statue of ice like man's despair.

It is the efforts of a child
Who made this image cold and wild
His mind made up his little hands
To build this thing on sterile lands.

A sexless heap of white abuse.
How can it be of any use?
Ice cold without, ice cold within,
It cannot judge, it cannot sin.

When the ultimate thaw begin,
It will grimace instead of grin;
And when the snow is washed away
It will survive for one more day.

To make an idiotic stand,
When all the snow has left the land;
The only white amid the green,
A relic of the winter scene.

And then it too will disappear,
Go forever, I know not where;
For it will leave without a nod
And maybe join its snowman god.

# HOME TOWN REYKJAVIK

Rising, cackling, on feet of pink
Above cold, Peter Black Sand;
Icy, rippling waters beneath,
Each ripple implanted with a
Heavenly light, supplied without
Charge, courtesy of the morning sun.

Gaining height, energising power,
Inventing strength, every sinew
Breathing in the oxygen of life.
Skeins a thousand, old and lately led,
Veteran campaigners and motley crew.
Home town Reykjavik, Godthab or
Svalbard Island.

Trisyllabic honking, haunting,
Contact seeking, keeping in vogue,
V-shapes, stately in the pink,
Norfolk sky. Skyward bound, to
Disappear, like magic, mid the
Bleak, rising dawn.
Solitude.

Sunset and they are back,
Distant voices, nearer, nearer,
Feeding over.
Back to their estriarine roost.
Gaggles a thousand yards wide,
A mile high, sixty thousand
Individuals a mile high, like
Kite strings broken from their bearers,
Flying free across the moon and stars,
Moving voices about the clouds
Left, right, all around, disappear like
Magic mid the bleak, rising gloom.

Our necks strained backwards,
We see them, we hear them. They
In their element, we in ours,
They drop in from the clouds, wheel
And arrive. Whiffling in descent.
Streams, streams! Songs of the wild
On the wind, like an orchestra
Gone mad!

Dream on wild geese, dream on
In your slumber. Dream of your
Northern flight that is to come.
Solitude.
Feather beds for your eggs. Dream on.
Rise at altitude to high latitudes.
Safe journey.
Home Town Reykjavik.

# THE WAY HOME

Rooks scamper across the even sky,
The leaden sky, laden with snow,
Anxiety is the road ahead;
The road ahead is all we know.

Night falls in, amid clamour and glare,
We head home with few stars alight.
A few miles to go, first flakes of snow;
Need to slow, as vision's not bright.

A barrage appears, millions of flakes,
Care with the brakes, home drawing nigh.
Crows settle in sleep, we just awake,
Snow scurrying high in the sky.

# WINTER NIGHT

The world is like a dead man,
So peaceful, cold and still;
Like one gigantic bed sheet
Stretched out across the hill.

As silent as a graveyard;
No whisper can be heard,
Except a piercing discord
From one old, cold blackbird.

The trees are now forgotten
Like soldiers battle worn,
They stand so still and silent,
So beaten and forlorn.

The snow lies deep and even
As snug as any glove,
And emphasises stillness
In earth and sky above.

Night falls upon the bed sheet,
A blanket on a bed,
A world of shattered silence,
A graveyard of the dead.

The world at last is sleeping,
No sorrow can be seen;
No noise of any battle,
No sign of village green.

The dead elms stand like martyrs,
Like tombstones dark and drear;
Like loved ones deep in mourning,
With shocks of greying hair.

The sun dies with a whimper,
Well beaten by the night;
And out across the hillside
A farmstead sheds a light.

The daylight's dying embers
Are less now than a spark;
White takes on a greyer tone.
For cometh now the dark.

The oaks melt with the sky line,
And heavy seems their sighs,
The ditches and the ridges
Blend in now with the skies.

This earth has much to offer
The rich man and the poor,
For soon will rise the morning
And soon will spring the thaw.

# WINTER COMES AND GOES

Rushing water, gushing water,
Gently rushing white,
Robin singing, sweetly singing,
Singing with delight.

Keys of ash all mellow, yellow,
Swaying in the air,
Children playing in clear water,
"Push me, if you dare!"

Restless skies above listless trees;
Green'ry fading fast,
Conifers all black and mystic
Waiting for the blast.

Nature waits with apprehension
For the sudden chill,
Snowflakes, glisten, strangely glisten
Glisten on the hill.

Winter comes with gay abandon,
All the fields are bare;
Here by magic paints a painter,
With exquisite care.

Winter rushing, winter dashing
Like a ball of snow,
Home fires burning, brightly burning,
O how they do glow.

Rushing water, gushing water,
Ice is breaking fast,
Robin singing, softly, singing,
Spring is here at last.

Gushing water gushing water
Gently rushing white
Robin singing, sweetly singing
Smiling with delight

Keys of ash all mellow yellow
Swaying in the air
Children playing in clear water
"Push me, if you dare"

Restless skies above listless trees
Greenery fading fast
Chillier, all black and mystic
Waiting for the blast

Nature waits with apprehension
For the sudden chill
Snowflakes glisten, sharply glisten
Glisten on the hill

Winter comes with gay abandon
All the fields are bare
Here by magic paints a painter
With exquisite care

Winter rushing, winter dashing
Like a ball of snow
Home fires burning, brightly burning
O how they do glow

Rushing water gushing water
Ice is breaking fast
Robin singing, softly singing
Spring is here at last

# CONFLICT

# THE POACHER'S MOON

It was the back end of October,
And the poacher's moon was bright,
Faded leaves had lost the birches,
The night was crisp and light.

The keepers were all ready,
Carefully worked out plans long laid
Now was the time to exploit them,
To outwit the poacher's ways.

For nights John and his father waited,
As the moon rolled through the skies,
Only to discover at daybreak,
Where the poacher took his prize.

Evidence suspiciously situated,
Near the bole of a lofty beech,
Up above blood-stained feathers cling,
Just out of keepers reach.

They were aware of his identity,
That was the easy part,
But how were they to catch him?
To beat him at his art.

They knew he used a pistol,
To bring the pheasants down,
As they peered silhouetted,
Against the poacher's moon.

The rogue was too crafty,
To take game home the same night,
He returned when the coast was clear,
To retrieve it from a dyke.

Shortly before midnight,
Father and son settled down,
To scan for the poacher's movements,
Like a tawny for a vole.

As they watched and chattered,
A jet soared towards the moon,
Then suddenly some lapwings rose,
From their ploughed-up farmland home.

The plovers' contrasting colours,
Created a beautiful picture far on high,
But what had caused their panic?
Was the poacher drawing nigh?

The keepers saw a figure move,
Dark image loomed up in the belt,
Would this be their tormentor?
Had their waiting been well spent?

Then they saw it's form quite clear,
And heard it's barking cry,
It was a handsome buck roe deer,
Outlined against the sky.

Again the watchers settled down,
Soon their patience was rewarded,
As the poacher came in sight,
His movements were recorded.

Old George was fascinating to watch,
Muttering in the gloom,
Stopping periodically,
Beneath the poacher's moon.

His bushy white hair shining,
Where moonbeams kiss the ground,
The keepers advanced towards him,
They dare not make a sound.

As they neared their quarry,
Moving on their hands and knees,
They were able to see quite clearly,
Old George amongst the trees.

He carried a plump cock pheasant,
Head pushed up under his belt,
The old birds long tail feathers,
A sight of sheer torment.

Young John and his father,
Were sure they'd got their man,
They both stood up together,
And shouted as George ran.

For years he'd been quick and artful,
But now his bones tired soon,
Which enabled the keepers to catch him,
Trapped beneath the poacher's moon.

# THE HUNT

Peace and quiet, awe of waiting,
Stirrup-cup and formal dating.
Thought of chase in hazy sunshine,
Red as red as red the skyline.

All the sinews, all the horses
Stretch and quake with heartfelt forces.
Steaming fetlocks, nostrils steaming,
Harness gleaming, riders beaming.

Fox is running, blood and thunder.
Who's for blood and who's for wonder?
Horn is blowing, hedges, ditches,
Curse the rich man for his riches.

Horse and hound and all together
Scramble, ramble, test their leather;
Pursue the varmint, wood and vale,
Yak, yap and yelp and yell and wail.

Hounds are winning closer action;
Bursting lungs and near exhaustion.
Tally-ho and master's bellow,
"It's a plucky little fellow!'

Fox is like a rag doll dying,
Breathless breath, no cry of crying,
Whoops of laughter, tittle-tattle,
Blackbird shrieks at cry of battle.

Peace and quiet, awe of waiting,
Stirrup-cup and formal dating,
Thought of chase in hazy sunshine,
Red as red as blood the skyline.

# THE TORMENTED WHALE

That great expanse of universe,
That none can hallow, none can nurse,
Has trapped within its volumes deep,
A broken soul that dares to sleep.
In blighted straits a devil waits;
And with sick joy it undertakes,
To gouge the vision of those eyes,
And throw up blood into the skies.
So torn with passion and with rage
The stricken soul fights in its cage,
To conquer that which man aspire,
To spite his ugly piece of wire.

# THE SACRILEGIOUS FIRE

In the distance I can see
A face without humanity.
Ants that crawl towards the fire
Have no chance now to retire;
And man himself has placed them there,
Far beyond what they can bear.

In the smoke a figure stands,
A figure without feet or hands;
Just one of nature's creatures,
A figure without features.
Oh where has gone the lunatic
Who perfected this sick trick?

Where has gone his big desire
To rescue nature from this fire?
He himself is doomed, it seems,
'Tis his fault that nature screams,
And 'tis his fault that ants perspire
On his sacrilegious fire.

# CHERNOBYL

O Chernobyl, I smell your breath,
The small lambs smell it too;
The pall of your untimely death
Has greyed our skies of blue.

Your poison chokes the silver fish
That dare to swim the sea;
And what a lethal, tasteless dish
Those silver fish will be.

You lurk within the very bones
Of mountain goats and men,
And mothers fret for little ones
They'll never see again.

We rue the nights our children dream
Of rabid Chernobyl,
And hope for days of pure sun-rays
On nature's velvet hill.

# EARTHQUAKE CITY

Where is this city,
This glorious city,
Gone with the dew
That fell on the hill.
Where are its people
Its wonderful people?
Crippled and shattered,
So silent and still.

Searchers are searching,
Like ants they are searching;
Near a dead child
A warrior found.
Stench of the stricken
Engulfs those that struggle,
Whores of the grottos
Have no one around.

Into the sky climbs
The pall of the horror
Out of each heart
There flows futile shame.
Where is the God who
Created the mountain?
O where is the love
That echoed his name.

# ABOVE THE WIND

Above the wind a cry I heard,
A cry not of a mortal bird;
The shriek I heard about my head
Was like a cry from someone dead.

And then again I heard that cry,
Like the spring of a broken toy:
Loss of sanity, loss of dress,
Crying out in the wilderness.

A soldier dying in a war?
The vision and the visitor?
And here along the street I see,
The victor and his victory.

The empty room where echoes roar
And no one cares about the poor:
Lonely, desperate, empty, blind
Are the souls of the human kind.

I close my eyes, a hand I see
Reaching down so desperately;
With fingers twisted, frail and white,
Illuminating this dark night.

Now searching eyes look down on me
And blink and stare and wink and cry,
Immortality shall I see,
Or will I fall where mortals lie?

# DIVISION

I'd rather live a joker than a knave,
I'd sooner die a sinner than a slave;
I'd sooner watch the stars and see the moon
Than bore away my life from morn till noon.
I'd sooner be a messenger of joy
Than ev'ry time I speak let out a cry:
But crying is the thing we ought to do,
For our world is divided into two.
The blood that runs through arteries and veins,
Differs in the politics it contains,
The holocaust that hangs about our heads
Will pluck us from our sleep and from our beds,
Unless we have the sense to overcome
The evil of division and the BOMB.

# BRITISH SOLDIER

British soldier in the battle
Far away from your homeland,
Fighting bravely for old Blighty
In the scorching desert sand.

We salute you and your number.
In our prayers we think of you.
With your courage and your valour
Fly the flag red, white and blue.

Little children all and sundry,
Innocence in spring sunshine.
They will grow into a future
As the strands of hope entwine.

You, our treasure, and our vision,
Rid the world of tyranny.
Our tomorrows will be brighter
Come the day of victory.

Come ye homeward British soldier,
To this free and fertile land,
To your loved ones waiting for you;
Heroes of the desert sand.

# SHADES OF LIFE

Men all the world over, love, laugh and cry.
We all live and love and then we all die.
The stars in the sky all fall in despair,
So why should we worry, why should we care?
The hungry crave for their next crust of bread;
Some of us wander in search of our dead.
Life can be cruel, like the cruel sea,
Some humans are caged whilst others are free.
Hist'ry repeats itself, men never learn.
Some nations look on as others just burn.
Our lives are a maze of myst'ry and woe,
It is hard to distinguish friend from foe;
And yet there is hope beyond what we see
And a propensity for what will be.

# FLOTSAM

I lie here without reason
And dream without a cause.
Time ticks away each season
Without a single pause.
No sense emerges from my dreams,
No remedies at all;
The messages run into streams;
Emerge without a call.

I look into a window,
A window without glass,
Believers all in situ
Lie stretched upon the grass.
This window of the world jets on
O'er valley, dale and hill
And the river floods with flotsam;
Nowhere the world is still.

The human race is runnng
Like ants within a wood,
No single factor winning,
No sentence understood.
The glass has smashed to smithereens:
The fragments lay around,
And the best of man's own thinking
Lies rotting in the ground.

## HUNG IN ROWS

Squirrel, weasel, owl and jay,
Use the beech wood ev'ry day;
All about the keepers' hut
Blood seeps down a buttercup.

Now the old crows croak no more,
For they dangle from barbed wire.
Bones do glisten in the sun,
Flesh and feather long since gone.

Magpie, hedgehog, hawk and jay,
Hang and sway from day to day.
Blood no more flows through their veins,
For they are the keeper's gains.

He crawls through the drains of life;
Like a man without a wife.
Cluttered up with torture tools,
Squeezing life from velvet moles.

I hear echoes, cries of pain
In each wooded field and lane.
From his hands the killing flows,
Rooks and crows are hung in rows.

Snare and trap and rifle butt,
Bullet where the skin is cut;
Poison where a life dries up,
Blood upon a buttercup.

# ANONYMOUS REFLECTIONS

All the way from my English lane,
To the city, I travel by train.
Up to see her beautiful face,
Now cold and dead in a peaceful place.

Down in the village talk is rife
About the carnage and loss of life.
Mid the anguish bouquets are laid;
Love will conquer, the flowers will fade.

Kill and be killed their anthem says
On one of London's bloodiest days.
They fly a flag as black as night;
It's up to us to lighten our plight.

As summer meets the autumn chill,
Berries ripen all over the hill;
And I, in anger, and repose
Will always cherish my English rose.

# THE BEGGAR-MAN

Beyond the river lies a grave
Where an old beggar fell,
And on a plaque are written words
Commending him to hell.

He paid his life for someone else,
So someone else could live;
He was a beggar-man alas,
With nothing else to give.

It happened at a lonely place,
Beyond a purple hill,
For that is where a young man died;
Where someone made a kill.

The beggar-man came walking past
The scene where John did die,
And went to see if all was well,
But then he heard a cry.

It was the sheriff's mighty men
With horses gleaming bright;
'Stand still' they said, 'You beggar-man.'
And then they did alight.

The court heard of this gruesome tale,
They hung the beggar old;
And on that sultry summer day,
The truth did not unfold.

The heather blooms around the grave,
The skylarks sing above;
Below the soil the beggar rots,
For his one act of love.

# THE WIND CALLS

Each time the wind calls in the pines
I think of someone dying,
I see a dreadful accident
And there a young man lying.
And when the wind moans in the dark
I see a ship in trouble,
I see a raft out on the sea
Where frightened sailors huddle.
I see a woman with a child,
Their hands raised in confusion,
I see a boat, a man afloat,
And this seems no illusion.
I hear a scream lost in the night,
A town smokes in the distance
And there another seems alight
Somewhere this very instance.

## THEY DIE

They die, the children die,
One by one they starve away.
In the southern sun they cry;
They suffer night and day.

Old men and women too
Are gripped by the self-same fate,
Swept on a tide of woe
Where death is never late.

There is no help for them
As no one has a care;
We will enjoy ourselves
And leave them dying there.

# LIFTING THE MARY ROSE

Our diver's found a cannon
An arrow and a bow;
Oh let us spend a million
And put them all on show.

Let's build a great museum
Where salt will fall a slave,
Rape old Mary in her tomb
And drag her from her grave.

And from her bony sailors
Let's rip off all their rags,
And steal away their treasures
In see-through plastic bags.

These bones, these bones, these old bones
Which sank into the deep,
Will shake again and shiver
When prodded from their sleep.

And when the sun of England
Warms them all through once more,
They'll be no mothers weeping
Or waving them ashore.

We'll have the ship resplendered
And clap our hands with glee;
Then show her to the people,
Our piece of history.

# DIFFERENT FACES

I look at his face when I'm angry
And see the love that is there;
Although he has been taken from us
I know his presence is near.

In this sacred homeland we bore him
And taught him right all along;
And he had the whole world before him,
Was clever, happy and strong.

They left him there bleeding and dying.
Hatred was not of his creed;
On a path in Eltham they found him,
Bigots had done their dire deed.

I look at his face when I'm angry
And see the hope that is there.
He rests in a faraway place now,
Far from injustice and fear.

This England, the home of all nations;
How dare you show off your face?
Racism is inscribed on your menu -
God knows there's only one race.

# DISTANT RACE

The night descends like immortality,
And claw upon the breast of humankind:
The forests whisper fruitless charity;
Although the players see, they are so blind.
And ev'ry creature that the world has known
Is like a carcass in the sun, flyblown.
Where crawls the dawn in this polluted cloud?
The distant race of limbs run heel to heel:
There must be somewhere one tree standing proud
To shudder but not fall to this ordeal.
And yet the poison falls again, and yet
The seeds are once more sown, the traps reset.
Deep in the humus of the human brain
Will ever love spring forth from fear again?

## MEMORIES OF WAR

The greenwood shows a mellow glint
As summer marches on,
The sky too, tells a diff'rent tale
For all the swifts have gone.
And old men wander down the lane
And there they reminisce;
They talk of days when they were young
So many miles from this.

They see the stubble-fields stretch out
Across the countryside
And visu'lise old battle-fields
Where comrades fell and died.
Those fine young men plucked in their prime
Like ears of tender corn,
Fell to the ground like bales of straw
Cut in the early morn.

The tanks stretched out like bales of straw
Mid the tolling thunder,
Bayonets bright, gleamed left and right,
Heroes all asunder.
And as the old men looked once more
Far beyond the combines,
They saw ten thousand grey gravestones
With crosses all in lines.

# FIRE BURNS FIRE

Drifting like a poison
Over the sinews of the brain;
Like a cataract slowly stealing
Across the surfaces of the mind.

Mists engulfs impressions made by
Cattle around the reservoir of life:
Even the innocent are polluted.

The lanes where flowers cry
Are soiled with soldiers blood.

The echo of a shadow dimly fades.

Shoes are worn upon the feet
Of a trodden down people,
Where lamps burn blind lights.

A canker gropes its way unmercifully,
Through valleys and terraced blocks,
Like a tarpaulin being whinced across
A cricket pitch.

Inevitably death follows hate.

The stench spews down, unstoppable,
Breaking up the colours of the garden.
Weeds stand guard where green vines stood.

The world seems a clouded image.
Men walk as if in a trance,
Hands filled with holes.
The streets they cross are divided,
Jealously guarded by faceless robots.

A child rises and calls,
Only to be trampled down;
Another rises, crying fades,
Great briars push up and choke.

Fire burns fire.

# DEATH FROM THE SKY

They fell like the autumn leaves,
Dead, all dead, and blown away,
Gone to early burials
On a sad September day.

Coffee slopped across the floor
As they gulped the acrid breath:
They'll not see their families -
Loving eyes are dulled in death.

A hydra-headed monster
Flew out of the rising sun,
A devil at its coat tails
And with evil to be done.

Candles glow and flags fly low;
Blooms bedeck the sooty street:
A rag doll lies so lonely
Now, amid fire-fighter's feet.

Prayers are said and tears are shed
There is outrage in the air,
They wake the sleeping giant
With a wrath beyond compare!

# THE VOICE OF MEMORY

Through the footprints and the echoes,
Skywards, upwards, never ending,
Ghosts unnumbered, some are resting.
Some are resting uncommitted,
And walk the stairs no longer there.

In a garden, sweet with roses
Loved ones ponder, terrafirma,
Wail and sigh, or barely murmur,
Old friends gone to meet their maker,
Those remaining lost in prayer.

# ELENI V

*(As recited on BBC radio)*


The seagull flew the waters calm,
Unaware of ensuing harm;
Then the crash of Eleni V
And crumpled feathers on the sea.

Its stomach burnt with grasping oil,
Engulfing seabird with the soil;
Gasping for breath it suffocates,
The price to pay for man's mistakes.

The tanker crashed and broke in two,
Her oil oozed out beneath the blue,
Where they mourned the Eleni V,
The dreaded junk yard of the sea.

Her filth laid stinking on the beach,
Where some of it was hard to reach;
A devil's slide rule stretched the shore,
Society's curse, like the whore.

She spewed her bowels out on the main,
Where oil clad creatures died in pain;
They moved her further, but in vain,
She spewed her guts up once again.

So rust in hell Eleni V;
Pathetic monster of the sea.
There you will rot for evermore,
Polluted fishes at your door.

# KOSOVO

Pottery pieces strewn over the land,
Scattered like fodder, the whim of a hand;
And lost components that fell by the way,
Some brightly coloured, some awfully grey.
So reminiscent when war is a tool.
When sorted they seem all part of the whole,
Discarded, broken and in disarray,
All hewn, it appears, from ord'nary clay
Mothers and elders and children in fear
Battle for mercy amid sore despair,
All with drawn faces and tears in their eyes,
With death all around and rage in the skies.
They flee the butcher who roars in Belgrade;
How, under heaven, was this monster made?

# THE DRUMS

The drums are beating loudly
On some far distant shore,
The cards are stacked against me
Far deeper than before,

On the wind my name is heard
In places far and wide -
Whisper, whispers everywhere,
I have no place to hide.

The net is closing in now,
A thief within the night,
I have no way to turn now,
I cannot see the light.

The traps were set to catch me,
I faulted for a while,
Then I fell into their snare;
They look to each and smile.

I must have been a big prize,
A big fish in their eyes.
I must have been a sharp thorn
Amid their piercing cries.

Their looks of satisfaction
Are sickening to see.
So now the drums beat loudly,
Beat loudly here for me.

# POPPY APPEAL

An old man came today
With poppies on display,
I picked one from his tray
And then he went away.

The poppy in my hand
Was not so very grand,
Just paper, understand!
Milled from another land.

Poppy Appeal, it said.
On black amid the red.
Red for the blood that shed
And black for all the dead.

For all dead that fell
Amid the bombs of hell
The brimstone and the smell
Where few came home to tell.

# IN NOVEMBER THE POPPIES LIE

In November the poppies lie
In dank and dismal days off-times
Neath Cenotaph and London sky,
Where sombre dress and muffled chimes
Denotes a nation's mournful mind
To remember kith, kin and kind.

Red as the autumn's sun, sets red,
Red as the blood of mortals - all:
We bow our heads to our dear dead
With thankful hearts we shall walk tall.
Red poppies with their empathy
With sacrifice and liberty.

In Flanders fields the poppies sway,
Each one a symbol of a face
Lost in the stench of Flanders' day,
Lost to defend our human race.
Their selfless act has set us free;
Their valour is our victory.

# WHEN THE TOY BREAKS

Her skies above are red with dust,
Her features black and bare.
Her ugly breast is scarred with rust;
Flames trample through her hair.
She lays there beaten, on her own,
Her broken heart can only moan,
And shake with mortal fear.

Her feet have ulcers pitted deep,
Her skin rejects the bone,
She weeps, she weeps and cannot sleep,
Her coffin drifts alone.
Her clothes are torn beyond repair,
The beast has poisoned his own lair
And now is vanquished, gone.

The voice she utters screams with pain,
Her hands are burnt away.
She will not walk nor talk again,
The oven burns her clay.
Her eyes are solid plastic bits
Upon her soul a devil sits
And laughs at her decay.

# DESERT FLOWERS

Flowers of the desert;
Flowers that bloom no more.
No blossom on their faces,
No blooms within their eyes.

All dried and fragmented,
Like broken bacon rind;
The desert winds have travelled
And have no love for them.

Their hands stretch outwards now
With eyes of sad renown.
Match-like are all their sinews,
As on their own they fall.

These desert flowers are bled,
And covered by the sand;
They die before the springtime,
Without a desert smile.

Those eyes say everything.
Although they speak no word;
Spring where is your miracle?
Where sings your summer bird?

# MASS GRAVE SOMEWHERE IN BOSNIA

They be then, there, all them that rot;
Wild flowers bloom as is their want.
They be then, there, at this sad spot,
And to the past the songbirds chant
For fallen loved ones, ev'ry one,
An epilogue in unison.

And those that mourn, howl in the dark;
Search in circles, and ramble far.
Poor souls that mourn, seek out a spark,
A sign, a light, a guiding star.
Where might they be? They cannot shout!
Where might they be, all them about?

They be then, there, all them that rot,
A shoe, a doll, marks this, their tomb.
They be then, there, neath this rough plot,
They never more to see their home.
Leaves flutter down in unison,
Spring, summer, autumn, - Winter soon!

## THOSE DISTANT LOVES or
## FALKLANDS REMEMBERED


Lost tombs of twisted elements
Wait vainly for deliverance.
Those distant loves reverberate,
They did not die for dying sake.

Those distant loves have ventured free
From gallows blowing in the sea,
Those sinews stricken in their prime
Arise again with strength divine.

They are not dead, these British men
They only sleep to rise again.
Their vict'ry flows triumphantly,
Their light to shine eternally.

Each heart will tug a mem'ry taught,
Each thought will free another thought
'Till mem'ries of a vacant kind
Induce the dulling of the mind.

Mankind must never let forget
Their sacrifice of blood and sweat;
Each spring will pull round spring anew
And moss will grow where no moss grew.

In the void of mist and motion,
Peace will climb above the ocean;
Then sink again behind its wake
And men will war for warring sake.

# THE SHUTTLE

Again, again, shuttle of the sky
Carries home the coldness of death.
Bearers await to raise each tomb
Above the soil of our heroes' birth.

The throng, steadfast, in sunshine and rain;
Coffins draped in red, white and blue.
The sign of death fronts, hat in hand.
Death for the many by the brave few.

Flags and banners fall in unison,
Blooms rain down as hearses pass by;
Loved ones cry out for loved ones gone;
Others too, will look towards the sky!